THE
TEN COMMANDMENTS
AND MODERN MAN

THE TEN
COMMANDMENTS
AND MODERN MAN

H. G. G. HERKLOTS

M.A. VICAR OF DONCASTER
HONORARY CANON OF SHEFFIELD

LONDON

ERNEST BENN LIMITED

First published 1958 by Ernest Benn Limited
Bouverie House · Fleet Street · London · EC4

© *H. G. G. Herklots 1958*

Printed in Great Britain

CONTENTS

Preface   *page* vii

Introduction   A God with a Name   9

I   None Other Gods   23

II   The Perils of Idolatry   32

III God's Name in Vain   53

IV   The Sabbath and the Stranger   66

V   Parents and Children   84

VI   The Sanctity of Life   96

VII The Sanctity of Marriage   115

VIII Reverence for Justice   132

IX   Telling the Truth   147

X   The Disease of Covetousness   166

Index of Scriptural References   181

Index of Names   187

PREFACE

A LITTLE while ago the Ten Commandments were being crowded out from Christian worship and given scanty attention in Christian thought and teaching. More recently we have come to realize what happens when the truths which they represent are neglected; and the Commandments are now attracting attention once again. A number of books have been published on the subject, of which Miss Joy Davidman's *Smoke on the Mountain* is the best known. My own interest was re-captured fifteen years ago by the Reverend John Drewett's *The Ten Commandments in the Twentieth Century* (S.P.C.K., 1941). There was at that time a note of challenge in the title. What had these ancient prohibitions to do with the modern world, it might have been asked, even with a world at war? To-day that title would seem natural enough. Had it not been already used it might have been employed for this book; for its endeavour is to examine the principles of the Decalogue afresh in the changing circumstances of this century.

The congregation at Doncaster Parish Church heard some of what is in this book in Lent 1956. Its writing was further stimulated by an invitation to give three public lectures at the University College of North Wales in November of the same year. My visit to Bangor was a most enjoyable one for me; and I greatly welcomed the opportunity to place some of my thoughts before a University audience. I am most grateful to Mr. D. R. Ap-Thomas and his committee for their invitation; and I recall with pleasure the gracious hospitality given me by the Reverend D. W. Gundry at Neuadd Reichel.

At the opening of each chapter I have set out the Commandment to be discussed, and a number of related biblical passages. As I have chosen these I have realized that their number might have been greatly increased; for very much of the Bible can be regarded as commentary on these simple formulations. I have added to each of these selections a prayer; which represents, I hope, the spirit in which I have tried to write, and in which I now offer this study of the Commandments to the public.

Doncaster   H. G. G. HERKLOTS
Lent, 1957

Introduction

A GOD WITH A NAME

I am the Lord thy God, which brought thee out of the land of Egypt, out of the house of bondage. *Exodus 20. 2.*

When Israel was a child, then I loved him, and called my son out of Egypt. *Hosea 11. 1.*

When thy son asketh thee in time to come, saying, What mean the testimonies, and the statutes, and the judgements, which the Lord our God hath commanded you? Then thou shalt say unto thy son, We were Pharaoh's bondmen in Egypt; and the Lord brought us up out of Egypt with a mighty hand. *Deuteronomy 6. 20–21.*

We have sinned with our fathers: we have done amiss and dealt wickedly.

Our fathers regarded not thy wonders in Egypt, neither kept they thy great goodness in remembrance: but were disobedient at the sea; even at the Red Sea.

Nevertheless, he helped them for his Name's sake: that he might make his power to be known. *Psalm 106. 6–8.*

Hungry and thirsty: their soul fainted in them.

So they cried unto the Lord in their trouble: and he delivered them from their distress.

He led them forth by the right way: that they might go to the city where they dwelt.

O that men would therefore praise the Lord for his goodness: and declare the wonders that he doeth for the children of men!

For he satisfieth the empty soul: and filleth the hungry soul with goodness. *Psalm 107. 4–8.*

These all died in faith, not having received the promises, but having seen them and greeted them from afar; and having confessed that they were strangers and pilgrims on the earth. *Hebrews 11. 13.*

O God, we have heard with our ears, and our fathers have declared unto us, the noble works that thou didst in their days, and in the old time before them.
O Lord, arise, help us, and deliver us for thine honour.

The Litany.

'YOU must get rid of that,' said the architect, standing at the east end of the Church and looking at the sombre plaques on which were set out the Ten Commandments, 'you must get rid of that – it's out of date.' When his hearers laughed he corrected himself, 'I didn't, of course, mean the Ten Commandments themselves.'

But many people in modern Britain have felt that it would be a good thing to abolish the Commandments altogether, which have been regarded as life-denying inhibitions. 'Let's get rid of them,' they have said, echoing the architect, 'let's get rid of them – they're out of date. Let's get rid of them, and bring some colour into life.'

In Christian worship also the recitation of the Commandments has become unfashionable. In the service of Holy Communion in the Church of England they are often replaced by hurried *Kyries*, 'Lord have mercy', which, the liturgiologists inform us, were the original material into which, at the Reformation, the alien Commandments were introduced. An even more common practice is to recite our Lord's summary of the Law and the Prophets. Here, indeed, time has brought a revenge. In the early centuries of the Christian era the Jews gave up the recitation of the Commandments because they were so popular among Christians, and substituted the *Shema*, from Deuteronomy:[1] 'Hear O Israel: the Lord our God, the Lord is one: and thou shalt love the Lord thy God with all thine heart, and with all thy soul, and with all thy might.' This is what Christians now repeat; though, following the example of Jesus, they have added to the original the word 'mind',[2] though this was a conception already implicit in the Hebrew original. Again, following the example of Jesus we have added the second commandment – which twentieth-century humanism so readily turns into the first – 'Thou shalt love thy neighbour as thyself.' But this is from Leviticus. We are still back in the Old Testament. The summary of the Law and the Prophets is taken from the Law itself.

There has been a revulsion also against manipulating the Commandments to meet the successive ethical needs of different centuries of Christian life. Thus the late Dr. W. R. Inge could complain in 1930: 'The absurd overvaluing of the Decalogue has left its traces in numberless old-fashioned churches in England as well as in other countries, where the Two Tables of the Law, along with the Creed and the Lord's Prayer, and sometimes even alone, occupy the east wall of the chancel.'[3] What was old-fashioned in the thirties of this century was new-fangled in the reign of the first Queen Elizabeth, when, in the *Order concerning Rood-Lofts*, issued in 1561, it was enjoined 'that there be fixed upon the wall, over the said communion board, the tables of God's precepts imprinted for the said purpose. Provided yet that in cathedral churches the tables of the said precepts be more largely and costly painted out, to the better show of the

[1] Ch. 6. 4–5.
[2] See Matt. 22. 37, Mark 12. 30, Luke 10. 27.
[3] *Christian Ethics and Modern Problems* (London, 1930), p. 227.

same.'[1] Are there any old-fashioned cathedrals left? No doubt their authorities have given a more modern interpretation to the Elizabethan words 'painted out'. In Archbishop Parker's famous *Advertisements* of 1566 order was also given 'to set the Ten Commandments upon the east wall over the said table.'[2]

Ingenious interpretation has not been confined to Protestants nor even to Christians. It was engaged in by Aquinas. A modern Jewish commentator on the Decalogue has written that 'the rabbis, as is to be expected, read into the Ten Commandments or out of them every noble human aspiration, every ideal that the prophets ever envisioned, and all the yearnings for brotherhood, peace, and communion with their Maker that welled up from the depths of their own piety.'[3] In recent years, however, the tendency has been rather to limit than to expand the implications of this ancient code. Thus Dr. Brunner has written, 'To use the Decalogue in the exposition of the Christian ethic is, of course, not prohibited, indeed, such use will always be an aim of Christian instruction. The Decalogue is eminently fitted to such use by its selection of the essential, by its incomparable arrangement and pregnancy. Hence it will always remain for us an unrivalled text for instruction, but not a source of insight into the truth of social ethics. When we wish to know what is just in the State, in economics, in society, marriage and the family, we receive no help from the Decalogue, but can only attach to its commandments what we have learned in other ways.'[4] The last sentence appears to be an over-statement. In the most complex situation a simple criterion may have relevance. One does not just add to the command *Thou shalt not steal*, except in the sense that a man adds to a foundation

[1] See *The Elizabethan Prayer-Book & Ornaments :* With an Appendix of Documents, by Henry Gee (London, 1902), p. 275.
[2] *Ibid.*, p. 272.
[3] Solomon Goldman, *The Ten Commandments* (Chicago, 1956), p. 77.
[4] *Justice and the Social Order* (London, 1954), p. 112.

by building upon it. What we have to do is to ask what these rules mean in the world of the twentieth century.

In the fifties of this century there has been little temptation to deplore the absurd overvaluing of the Decalogue. Earlier decades might be attracted by Kipling's semi-mythical realm somewhere East of Suez, where 'there ain't no ten commandments': to-day the very place-names Sinai and Suez emphasise the lack of an international code of behaviour, without which the nations are likely to perish. Or do we all agree with a leader-writer in the *Daily Mail*,[1] that 'In international affairs there is, in the ultimate, no moral conscience'? Nationally, a culture which rejects the discipline of the Commandments for the pursuit of hedonism is not likely to make a great contribution to the world. The mood of to-day induces a nostalgic recollection of days when boys and girls learned these great prohibitions by heart, not necessarily understanding them, but giving them a place in the unconscious mind whence they might effectively censor and control. 'In England, perhaps alone amongst the world's most populous countries,' it has been recently written, 'politics are not looked on by the man in the street as on the whole rather dirty, a fact it would be hard to account for unless the old ruling class had political sagacity and if the best of them had not taken politics seriously.'[2] Might not this also be related to a Decalogue set out and taught in old-fashioned churches?

The critic might say that this was a source also of the notorious British hypocrisy in foreign politics, to say nothing of the nervous breakdowns which are so common. 'There is no doubt,' writes a psychologist, 'that a vast amount of psychogenic misery is caused by this setting of too high a standard for one's self, and the fact that the great majority of

[1] August 14, 1956.

Uncommon People, A Study of England's Elite, by Paul Bloomfield (London, 1955), p. 184.

those who suffer in this way have never called in question, or indeed explicitly recognised, that they expect more from themselves than they do from others shows both the extent of their primitive narcissism and the degree to which this narcissism has been displaced from the real ego to the ego-ideal.' The same writer remarks, 'So long as we regard ourselves as dabblers, amateurs, dilettanti, or beginners we feel we cannot seriously be blamed or despised, that we cannot even blame or despise ourselves, for inferior performances. . . . If we are to aim consistently at the highest of which we are capable, we must continually exert ourselves to the utmost. But in so far as we pitch our aspirations to a lower key, we may quite legitimately and quite realistically console ourselves for the little showing we have made by the thought that we could have done more had we chosen to make the necessary effort.'[1]

This advice would hardly have suited Saul of Tarsus, who could never have brought to life the attitude which is legitimate towards a hobby. So far as life itself is concerned we are none of us amateurs, but all professionals. But the psychogenic misery consequent upon the endeavour to keep a law points to the need for that which is beyond and above law. A Christian commentator on the Ten Commandments must constantly look from them to the One whose coming not only fulfilled the Law and the Prophets but also released the power which was needed for the achievement of the Law's ideals. 'If there had been a law given which could have given life, verily righteousness should have been by the law.'[2] Paul's interior distress was a cross born for others, who can be taught, early in their Christian progress, that where law fails grace can be effective; but who, no matter what they have been taught, most often have to make the great discovery for themselves.

[1] J. C. Flugel, *Man, Morals and Society* (London, 1955), pp. 62, 87, 88.
[2] Gal. 3. 21.

Certainly the compilers of the Book of Common Prayer intended that the Commandments should play a great part in the life of England; that they should be for all men's behaviour a standard of reference. At a Baptism the Godparents were reminded twice of their duty:

and chiefly ye shall provide, that he may learn the Creed, the Lord's Prayer, and the Ten Commandments, in the vulgar tongue, and all other things which a Christian ought to know and believe to his soul's health.

And again:

Ye are to take care that this child be brought to the Bishop to be confirmed by him so soon as he can say the Creed, the Lord's Prayer, and the Ten Commandments, in the vulgar tongue, and be further instructed in the Church Catechism set forth for that purpose.

When we turn to the Catechism itself, we find the Commandments set out once again, with an interpretation which relates the first four to our duty towards God and the last six to our duty to our neighbour. The Larger Catechism, composed by the Puritan divines sitting at Westminster between 1643 and 1647 also makes the same division – 'the four first Commandments containing our duty to God, and the other six our duty to man' – and in the same assembly's Shorter Catechism it is also implicit. It was the agreement of that age, substantiated by the agreement of many ages of antiquity, that in the Commandments the Moral Law was 'summarily comprehended'.[1] The Roman Catholic Church, in the Catechism prepared by the Council of Trent, also declared that 'our ancestors have wisely reduced the whole force and system of the doctrine of faith to these four heads: the Apostles' Creed, the Sacraments, the Ten

[1] The Larger Catechism.

Commandments, and the Lord's Prayer.'[1] In the Charity Schools, which had a great influence upon England in the eighteenth century, the whole of education was based upon Catechism, Bible, and *The Whole Duty of Man*.[2] When this last volume is examined it is found also to be closely linked with the Commandments.

From the standpoint of to-day the world of yesterday appears contained and static, a world of men who naturally accepted a static code. Those were the days of certainties, we feel: now all is uncertain. But the contrast between static and dynamic conceptions of living is not now being worked out for the first time in human history. When life has passed its meridian it is natural to recall and to regret the years when recognised landmarks had not been disturbed, when order seemed still to be recognised and revered, the days before chaos was king —

> *Before this strange disease of modern life*
> *With its sick hurry, its divided aims,*
> *Its heads o'ertax'd, its palsied hearts, was rife.*

The fact that Matthew Arnold published *The Scholar Gipsy* in 1855, just after income-tax had been doubled – from sevenpence to one and twopence in the pound – is a reminder that nostalgia as well as hope springs eternal in the human breast. 'Change and decay in all around I see,' proclaims one, while another replies, 'Nothing of the sort. Life involves change. Change makes for progress. And the possibilities of progress, if only people will be sensible and not smash the whole show up, are illimitable.' So men break away from the static society, where everyone is thought to have his place, his just remuneration, his special clothing even, fitted to his station in life, the society in which people

[1] Quoted, John Baillie, *The Idea of Revelation in Recent Thought* (London, 1956), p. 30.

[2] See Dorothy Marshall, *English People in the Eighteenth Century* (London, 1956), p. 161.

believed that there was an eternal pattern of law, laid up in the heavens, perhaps, but not wholly unrecognisable on earth. Thus Hooker could write of Law that 'her seat is the bosom of God, her voice the harmony of the world: all things in heaven and earth do her homage, the very least as feeling her care, and the greatest as not exempted from her power: both Angels and men and creatures of what condition soever, though each in different sort and manner, yet all with uniform consent, admiring her as the mother of their peace and joy.'[1] At a very great remove, also, but of no little importance in forming the minds of a generation of Englishmen, Rudyard Kipling was continually appealing to the conception of a Law which demanded the allegiance of right-thinking men, but which was perhaps more certainly obeyed, and more clearly exemplified, in the jungle than in human life.

At the present time a return to the Commandments might be no more than nostalgic, the natural conservatism of the 'fifty plus' age-group. But it could be more important. 'Exodus XX is timeless,' writes Dr. T. H. Robinson, 'and its provisions are valid for any conditions of organised human society.'[2] If this be true, then few things could be more important than that we should examine those provisions again; that there should not be a thin trickle of books on the subject but a swelling flood. There is no static condition of society to which we can return. But if there are principles to guide us in an uncertain future, whether it be of disaster or achievement, it were well for us to probe them afresh that we may understand them better.

The Decalogue is hardly a code of behaviour for atheists, nor even for agnostics. It involves a presupposition which is

[1] *Laws of Ecclesiastical Polity* I. xvi. 8. quoted *The National Church and the Social Order* (Westminster, 1956), p. 14.

[2] W. O. E. Oesterley & T. H Robinson, *A History of Israel* (Oxford, 1932), vol. i, p. 96.

too easily taken for granted by Christian speakers and writers, what Professor H. A. Hodges has called 'the Abrahamic presupposition.'

'Abraham in the story is a man who has committed himself unconditionally into the hands of God; a man who does what God asks of him without hesitation, however paradoxical or self-contradictory it may seem, and who accepts God's promises, however mysterious and incredible they may appear. It is by virtue of this unconditional self-commitment to God that he has won the title of the Friend of God. But such an attitude evidently presupposes a great deal. It presupposes not merely the existence of God, about which the philosophers have debated so lengthily, but that God is of a certain character. It presupposes that God has complete control of the world and the course of events in it; that He exercises this control in a way which is purposeful; that human beings have a place in His designs; and that He communicates with them in ways which they can legitimately understand as commands and promises, and by which their lives can be guided. This is the presupposition of Jewish and Christian thinking, which I call Abrahamic theism.'[1]

Nor is this all. The origin of the Commandments is placed by the Hebrew writers at a particular time in their national history, within what they believed to be a particular experience of God's communication. It is the fundamental Christian belief that God has spoken – that 'God, who at sundry times and in divers manners spake in time past unto he fathers by the prophets, hath in these last days spoken unto us by his Son.'[2] The fathers, for Christian and for Jew, are the Hebrew peoples whom God chose for a particular

[1] *Christianity and the Modern World View* (London, 1949), p. 28.

[2] Heb. 1. 1, 2.

destiny; that they might be the means of His communication with all mankind.

Most of the peoples of the ancient world believed that their relationship to their god was natural and inescapable. They were descended from him; therefore they were his people. But what is shewn in Exodus is different: it is the choice by Israel of the Lord as their God; a response to His choice of Israel as His people; an acceptance of an artificial compact by which both sides were pledged. It has been said that one sentence sums up the whole history of the religious life of Israel, 'I will become their God, and they shall become my people.'[1] This mutually accepted choice is described by Hebrew writers as making a covenant. The conception has behind it the practice by which desert tribes enlarged their numbers by taking other tribes into formally-enacted blood relationships with each other, a process intended to provide permanent freedom from the hazards of politics and the mutability of political alliances. The Hebrew phrase to 'cut' a covenant suggests the physical acts which were associated with the establishment of covenant relationships between tribes.[2] At Sinai God entered into a covenant relationship with the Hebrews. The Commandments represent in brief – and originally they were doubtless briefer still – the ethical standards accepted by Israel as the covenant people of God. The words with which they are introduced are not an irrelevant extra: they are an essential certification. *I am the Lord thy God, which brought thee out of the land of Egypt, out of the house of bondage.*[3] Israel knew God first as a deliverer. It was to this deliverance from Egypt that prophets and psalmists looked back. The deliverance, and the obedience to God's will associated with it, were what constituted

[1] Cf. Lev. 26. 12.

[2] Cf. R. B. Y. Scott, *The Relevance of the Prophets* (New York, 1944), pp. 22, 23.

[3] Exod. 20. 2.

Israel a separate nation. True Israelites could never forget the Red Sea and Sinai. Wherever they settled their memories went back; and their religious ceremonies were designed to jog their memories.

This sort of thing, for example, used to happen at a harvest festival:

> 'And the priest shall take the basket out of thine hand, and set it down before the altar of the Lord thy God. And thou shalt answer and say before the Lord thy God, A Syrian ready to perish was my father, and he went down into Egypt, and sojourned there, few in number; and he became there a nation, great, mighty, and populous; and the Egyptians evil entreated us, and afflicted us, and laid upon us hard bondage: and we cried unto the Lord, the God of our fathers, and the Lord heard our voice, and saw our affliction, and our toil, and our oppression; and the Lord brought us forth out of Egypt with a mighty hand, and with an outstretched arm, and with great terribleness, and with signs, and with wonders; and he hath brought us into this place, and hath given us this land, a land flowing with milk and honey. And now, behold, I have brought the first of the fruit of the ground, which thou, O Lord, hast given me.'[1]

The Hebrews exalted Law, but it was never for them a dead code: it was always evidence of the activity of the living God; and the setting of the Ten Commandments indicates that within His activity His will and His nature are revealed. God confronts man, not with an argument for His existence but with a proclamation of His will. Yet with the potency of command is mingled the warmth of invitation:

> 'O taste and see that the Lord is good:
> Blessed is the man that trusteth in him.'[2]

[2] Deut. 6. 5–10.　　　　[1] Psalm 34. 8.

The Old Testament words provide means for the Christian evangel. For it is the same God with whom Old and New Testament are both concerned.

What we are saying, in modern terms, is that there is no religious experience without risk – without the risk of being wrong. The greatest ventures in life – marriage, for example, or entering a profession – have to be made upon insufficient evidence. Yet the venture of faith is made. In our day an increasing number of thinking men and women are accepting Professor Hodges' 'Abrahamic presupposition', which, as he says, 'differs in obvious ways from the scientific presupposition, but it has the same logical properties and status. It is not a self-evident truth, nor a piece of knowledge gathered from experience, but a presupposition made as a result of a basic acceptance. It is prejustified because it enables us to open up a field of experience which cannot be opened up without it, and discoveries in which, if made, would have a close bearing on human interests. It gives facts a new significance, and raises questions and gives rise to theories of a distinctive kind. Its postjustification lies in the fact that theories do arise in this field which cover the known facts, point the way for further inquiries and fresh discoveries, and enable us to act in ways which are important and beneficial.'[1]

It is only for those who have made this basic acceptance that the Ten Commandments are personally relevant. Here ethics cannot be dissociated from theology, nor behaviour from obedience to the living God who stands behind the human words in which men have discovered His will. Many of the prohibitions of the Decalogue are, of course, accepted by men of good will who deny belief in God. 'Murder, adultery, theft and slander are still condemned by the modern world in theory, if not always in practice, whilst most people would admit that covetousness lies at the root of

[1] *Op. cit.*, p. 29.

more than one of the other offences.'[1] But if there be a feeling
of obligation in the matter, something different from the
agreement that this is a sensible way to behave, it is the relict
of a once dominant theism, and its maintenance is, in the last
resort, derivative.

The central teaching of the Book of Genesis is that God
is Creator. The world is His, however much men may rebel
against Him, however disastrously they may mar the place
He has given them to occupy and develop. The central
teaching of the Book of Exodus is that He is also Deliverer.
Already He has begun His pilot experiment through a chosen
people. *I am the Lord thy God, which brought thee out of the
land of Egypt, out of the house of bondage.* Here are two lessons
which the world needs to re-learn. The first is that God is
active in history. He is not above us in the sense of being unconcerned in our doings. He is vitally concerned. Our
decisions are of moment to Him. The easy cry of to-day is
'What does it matter?' That is not a question a Christian can
ask, nor anyone nurtured in that religious inheritance from
which Christianity sprang. The Old Testament is a record of
God at work; of God standing beside men who have the
courage to put their trust in Him. Secondly, He is a God with
a name. *I am the Lord thy God*, we read; and the word 'the
Lord' stands for the name which early English translators
rendered Jehovah (though it was probably sounded *Yahweh*).
People nowadays often say, 'Well, I suppose there's something behind it all' – but something behind it all is not a
God with a name. We do not often call God Jehovah, because we know Him as Father. But already on Mount Sinai
He was revealed as personal; one whom men could approach, whom they could please or displease: and in that
personal nature there is to be detected the possibility of
personal religion.

[1] T. H. Robinson in *The Old Testament and Modern Study* (London,
1951), p. 356.

I

NONE OTHER GODS

Thou shalt have none other gods before me. *Exodus 20. 3.*

The whole world before thee is as a grain in a balance, and as a drop of dew that at morning cometh down upon the earth. But thou hast mercy on all men. *Wisdom of Solomon 11. 21, 22.*

Hast thou not known? hast thou not heard, the everlasting God, the Lord, the Creator of the ends of the earth, fainteth not, neither is weary; there is no searching of his understanding. He giveth power to the faint; and to him that hath no might he increaseth strength. Even the youths shall faint and be weary, and the young men shall utterly fall: but they that wait upon the Lord shall renew their strength; they shall mount up with wings as eagles; they shall run and not be weary; they shall walk and not faint. *Isaiah 40. 28–31.*

O the depth of the riches both of the wisdom and the knowledge of God! how unsearchable are his judgements, and his ways past tracing out! For who hath known the mind of the Lord, or who hath been his counsellor? Or who hath first given to him, and it shall be recompensed again? For of him, and through him, and unto him are all things. To him be the glory for ever. Amen.
Romans 11. 33–36.

And this is the message which we have heard from him, and announce unto you, that God is light, and in him is no darkness at all. *1 John. 1. 5.*

Behold, the tabernacle of God is with men, and he shall dwell with them, and they shall be his people, and God himself shall be with them, and be their God. *Revelation 21. 3.*

O God, who hast prepared for them that love thee such good things as pass man's understanding; Pour into our hearts such love toward thee, that we, loving thee above all things, may obtain thy promises, which exceed all that we can desire; through Jesus Christ our Lord. Amen.

Collect for the sixth Sunday after Trinity.

———

I am the Lord thy God, which brought thee out of the land of Egypt, out of the house of bondage. Thou shalt have none other gods before me. This commandment, as originally set out and as originally received, does not deny the existence of other gods besides Yahweh, God of Israel. The Hebrew people passed from a belief in many gods to the belief that there was only one God who mattered, to the final belief in the existence of one God only, maker of Heaven and earth. The latter stages of this development are reflected in the Jewish interpretation of this commandment. It proclaimed monolatry but was interpreted as being monotheistic. This interpretation the Christian Church inherits; and this we naturally accept. But it would be hypocrisy to pretend that the ordinary Israelite was a natural monotheist. David understood his exile from the land of his fathers as one which bade him 'Go serve other gods.'[1] When Naaman the Syrian was cured of his leprosy by dipping in the waters of Jordan he wanted to serve the God of Israel for ever. What was needed if he was to do this in a foreign country? He must have some Israelite earth on which to stand: 'Let there be given to thy servant two mules' burden of earth; for thy servant will henceforth offer neither burnt offering nor sacrifice unto other gods but unto the Lord.'[2] Elisha did not reply that a

[1] 1. Sam. 26. 19.   [2] 2. Kings 5. 17.

man could worship Yahweh anywhere, because He was Lord of all the ends of the earth. What he said was, 'Go in peace.' The First Commandment does not deny the existence of other gods: it forbids them to be worshipped.

This illogical position led in the end to a complete rejection of belief in the existence of any gods except their own, who was not theirs only, but God of all the world. 'Thus saith the Lord, the King of Israel, and his redeemer the Lord of hosts: I am the first, and I am the last; and beside me there is no God.'[1] For the time being His most intimate concern was with one people, but His mercy embraced all men, and He was using the one people of the Hebrews to make known that mercy to all men.

'Declare ye, and bring it forth; yea, let them take counsel together: who hath shewed this from ancient time? who hath declared it of old? have not I the Lord? and there is no god else beside me; a just God and a saviour; there is none beside me. Look unto me, and be ye saved, all the ends of the earth: for I am God, and there is none else. By myself have I sworn, the word is gone forth from my mouth in righteousness, and shall not return, that unto me every knee shall bow, every tongue shall swear.'[2]

The Israelites must only think of themselves as specially provileged when they recalled that privilege always implied responsibility. The remembrance of deliverance should always be a stimulus to responsibility. 'Hear this word that the Lord hath spoken against you, O children of Israel, against the whole family which I brought up out of the land of Egypt, saying, You only have I known of all the families of the earth: therefore I will visit upon you all your iniquities.' So wrote Amos.[3] And again: 'Are ye not as the children of the Ethiopians unto me, O children of Israel? saith the Lord.

[1] Isaiah 44. 6.   [2] Isaiah 45. 21–23.   [3] Amos 3. 1, 2.

Have not I brought up Israel out of the land of Egypt, and the Philistines from Caphtor, and the Syrians from Kir?'[1] Underlying the progress from monolatry to monotheism there lay the hope of a coming time when the Lord would destroy 'the face of the covering that is cast over all peoples, and the veil that is spread over all nations.'[2] The hope of a world Church has its roots deep in the Old Testament revelation.

This progress was made in a world where religious beliefs remained polytheistic and static. Polytheism is not merely an unsatisfactory belief. It is a dangerous one; and for three reasons. In the first place one who believes in many gods has no ultimate security. He never knows where he is. There may always be some vengeful divinity whom he has forgotten to propitiate or of whose existence he was unaware. It is very questionable whether modern science could have arisen in the chancy world of polytheism. Scientific research, as A. N. Whitehead pointed out, rests upon the 'belief that every detailed occurrence can be correlated with its antecedents in a perfectly definite manner exemplifying general principles,' and this belief came from 'the medieval insistence on the rationality of God, conceived of as with the personal energy of Jehovah and with the rationality of a Greek philosopher.'[3] There is no certain moral order to which a polytheist can appeal: there is a moral disorder; a pattern placed upon chaos by the one who claims to be in the know, the witch-doctor or medicine man. But even he may not put all his gods in the shop window; may be holding some supernatural power in reserve to use for selfish ends.

In the second place a believer in many gods has no ultimate sense of responsibility. As, on the one hand, he

[1] Amos 9. 7.

[2] Isaiah 25. 7.

[3] Science and the *Modern World*, quoted Leonard Hodgson, *For Faith and Freedom* (Oxford, 1956), p. 8.

may be at the mercy of an unknown or unpropitiated divinity, so, on the other, he may himself change his allegiance. This happened to a very great extent when the Hebrew tribes entered Palestine. Yahweh, to whom they had covenanted themselves at Sinai, might be supreme in the wilderness or on the hills; but in the new agricultural life of the rich land they had entered, and in the towns, His worship seemed out of place. It was natural to find out all about the local gods, who should be propitiated when a good harvest of grapes or figs was desired. This situation lies behind the whole conflict over Baal which plays so large a part in the historical books of the Old Testament: the baals were mostly the local fertility gods, who were thought of as the source of good harvests; and who were worshipped with immorality and drunkenness. The prophet Hosea, in the name of Yahweh, could complain about a disobedient people, who behaved like an ungrateful wife: 'She did not know that I gave her the corn, and the wine, and the oil, and multiplied unto her silver and gold, which they used for Baal. Therefore will I take back my corn in the time thereof, and my wine in the season thereof, and will pluck away my wool and my flax which should have covered her nakedness.'[1]

In the third place, polytheism brings with it a lowered conception of the goodness of God. Belief in God's holiness, as it is found in Isaiah, depends upon belief in His supremacy. Where gods are thought to exist in competition with one another there is introduced into men's conception of their life the competitiveness of human existence. In Greece the philosophers regarded with a smiling tolerance which was near to contempt the activities of the Olympians. Jewish apologists for their faith in the Hellenistic world wrote Greek treatises to show that through Judaism alone there was to be encountered a God of whom Greek philosophers could approve. When a man believes in many gods

[1] Hosea 2. 8, 9.

them, almost of necessity, possess the attributes
ten associated with devils.

not the purpose of this book to set out arguments for
belier in God. It is relevant, however, to our subject to consider what happens when belief in God decays: though
Christian apologists must always beware lest they commend
belief in God because that belief is useful, because it serves to
maintain social unity and to prevent revolution. In the end
these efforts defeat themselves. Belief in God does not remain an effective force when it is only propagated because it
is good for morale. Nevertheless, it needs to be pointed out
that where people cease to believe in one God they are likely
to develop a semi-conscious belief in many. In the modern
West, where the Abrahamic presupposition is effectively
held by fewer people, the weaknesses associated with
polytheism clearly emerge. People feel insecure: they do not
know what or whom to trust: they feel that the Universe has
let them down. Meanwhile, through charms and mascots
and gremlins – if not actually goblins – the old gods make
their return. 'You never know,' people say, 'there may be
something in it.' Coupled with this is a sense of irresponsibility; of not belonging; of not being responsible to any certain code; of having no ultimate loyalty. Goodness itself
becomes relative. Quick pleasures are sought rather than
long-term satisfactions. 'Let reverence for God and moral
order go and life has lost that which gives it meaning and
stability. That is the abiding truth in the first Commandment.'[1]

*I am the Lord thy God . . . thou shalt have none other gods
before me.* In the personal life of many God has ceased to be a
reality – and life has lost its grandeur, becoming little more
than a competitive scramble for existence, while we accept
and enjoy the good things which a pleasure-loving society
has to offer. This retreat from theism has taken place not

[1] A. R. Osborn, *Christian Ethics* (London, 1940), p. 143.

only in individual life: it has dominated the wide sweep of world politics, so that the fragile framework of Christendom has been broken, and new divisions separate mankind. To say that the world is in God's hands is one thing: to say that it is at the mercy of inscrutable forces is another; and between the two there is the difference between security and insecurity. Many declare that human development is governed almost entirely by economic forces; and that in consequence the future is predictable; and the ultimate victory of the proletarian class assured. The dogmatic assurance of Communism can be very attractive; and those who profess its creed have often the faith and hope, if not the charity, which marked the early Christians. But a certainty that has to be enforced by bayonets and purges and a secret police comes in time to have a rather uncertain look; and Communism deals as hardly with its heretics as any creed in history. Elsewhere, first in Europe and then with increased force in Asia and Africa, there has been an eruption of nationalist passions, demanding an absolute loyalty. The First Commandment declares that an absolute loyalty is rightly given to God alone.

Christians have long realised that the challenge to their beliefs is a fundamental one. It is significant that when Dr. Martin Niemöller, at the height of his conflict with the Nazi authorities before the Second World War, published a volume of the sermons which had caused such offence, its English title was *First Commandment*.[1] The English reader did not immediately discern anything very remarkable about them. They were biblical sermons; that was all. And that was enough. Acceptance of the biblical revelation is a direct contradiction of the belief that the state should be given an absolute loyalty, that the state alone, in the final resort, can decide what is right and what is wrong. This remains the fundamental conflict of to-day; a conflict within

[1] London, 1937.

democratic countries as well as between them and totalitarian régimes.

In 1937, the ecumenical Conference on Church, Community and State, held at Oxford, declared with a forboding prescience:

'The Church is under obligation to proclaim the truth that the disintegration of society has one root cause. Human life is falling to pieces because it has tried to organize itself into unity on a secularistic and humanistic basis without any reference to the divine Will and Power above and beyond itself. It has sought to be self-sufficient, a law unto itself. Nor is there any hope in the ascription of sacred quality to the nation or State or class. A false sacred, a false God merely adds demonic power to the unredeemed passions of men. Though bringing about temporary and local unity it prepares for mankind an even worse and wider conflict. The recall to God in penitence must stand first.'[1]

Elsewhere in the same report it was noted that 'Centres of economic power have been formed which are not responsible to any organ of the community and which in practice constitute something in the nature of a tyranny over the lives of masses of men.'[2] Man, it would appear, is made to be mastered. If he does not accept the mastery of the God who made him he may well find himself mastered by forces he has himself set in motion but cannot control. Christians believe that God invites men into a service which is perfect freedom: it is becoming a widespread experience that human promises of freedom tend to depress men into servitude.

In subsequent deliverances of the World Council of Churches the nature of this challenge has been more exhaustively explored. Thinking Christians are without excuse

[1] *The Churches Survey Their Task* (London, 1937), p. 68.
[2] *Ibid.*, p. 88.

if they are unaware that the conflict between Christianity and its adversaries is not a passive one; and that God demands in our day a loyalty which is complete and disciplined.

I am the Lord thy God. A Christian believes that man is not at the mercy of the impersonal and the unpredictable. There is no mere President of the Immortals toying with his puppets. God has a Name. The Hebrews called Him Yahweh; though that Name was too holy for them ever to utter in human speech. Because of what he has learned from Jesus Christ a Christian can go further and call God his Father – though it would be well if he could reproduce sometimes a fraction of that sense of awe which devout Jews still feel when they approach the Name of God. It is possible to be too familiar with our Maker. The Christian does well to look back to Sinai. Indeed early Christians looked back further still, to the deliverance from Egypt which they regarded as pre-figuring the deliverance through Jesus Christ. The traditional Sinai is a most impressive place. 'Whatever may have been the scene of the events in Exodus,' wrote Dean Stanley, 'I cannot imagine that any human being could pass up that plain and not feel that he was entering a place above all others suited for the most august of the sights of the earth.'[1] Golgotha can hardly be so impressive. But they are peaks in the same spiritual range. The revelation on Golgotha takes the believer further and deeper than the revelation on Sinai; for the Second Covenant fulfilled and replaced the first. But had there been no first Covenant there might have been no second. The Christian has a great inheritance. But it is not one to occupy and enjoy. It is an inheritance that equips him for service.

[1] *Sinai and Palestine* (London, 1866), p. 75

II

THE PERILS OF IDOLATRY

Thou shall not make unto thee a graven image, nor the likeness of any form that is in heaven above, or that is in the earth beneath, or that is in the water under the earth: thou shalt not bow thyself to them, nor serve them: for I the Lord thy God am a jealous God, visiting the iniquity of the fathers upon the children, upon the third and upon the fourth generation of them that hate me; and shewing mercy unto thousands of them that love me and keep my commandments. *Exodus 20. 4–6.*

Return ye, and turn yourselves from all your transgressions; so iniquity shall not be your ruin. Cast away from you all your transgressions, wherein ye have transgressed; and make you a new heart and a new spirit: for why will ye die, O house of Israel? For I have no pleasure in the death of him that dieth saith the Lord God: wherefore turn yourselves and live.

Ezekiel 18. 30–32.

Therefore also among the idols of the nations shall there be a visitation, because, though formed of things which God created, they were made an abomination, and stumbling blocks to the souls of men, and a share to the feet of the foolish.

Wisdom of Solomon 14. 11.

The hour cometh, and now is, when the true worshippers shall worship the Father in spirit and truth: for such doth the Father seek to be his worshippers. God is a Spirit: and they that worship him must worship in spirit and truth. *John 4. 23, 24.*

Giving thanks unto the Father, who made us meet to be partakers of the inheritance of the saints in light; who delivered us out of the power of darkness, and translated us into the kingdom

the whole law.'[1] Nor is this emphasis out of date. 'Modern
missionaries in first contact with inquirers have to lay down
firmly at the start some things which cannot be permitted
if they would be Christians. The beginning is probably the
same, idolatry.'[2] When St. John wrote, 'little children, guard
yourselves from idols,' his meaning, says Professor Dodd,
was 'avoid any contact with paganism.' The Greek word for
idols (*eidola*), he tells us, 'always carries with it the suggestion of unreality. Plato used it for the illusory phenomena or
appearances which he contrasted with the eternal and im-
mutable "ideas" or "forms". In the Greek Old Testament
the same word was adopted to designate the images worshipped by the heathen, as being counterfeit gods over
against the one real God. In this sense it was taken over by
Christianity.'[3] The early Christians had the Jewish horror of
images. A modern Christian, if he were transported to first
century Athens, might find himself thrilled by the profusion of
noble statuary. Paul revealed his upbringing when 'his spirit
was provoked within him, as he beheld the city full of idols.'[4]

This was, however, the end of a very long process, and the
formulation of the Second Commandment, as we now have
it, probably came from a late date. When there was a plague
of serpents in the wilderness Moses himself interpreted it as
God's command to make a brass serpent, and set it upon a
standard as a talisman against danger.[5] It was hundreds of
years before this, or its successor, was removed from the
Temple by Hezekiah, because it had become an object of
superstitious veneration.[6] Until the Exile in Babylon the
ideal of worship without the use of images differed widely
from the actual practice. We remember how at the foot of

[1] *Sifre*. Num. sect. 111, Deut., sect. 54, quoted G. F. Moore, *Judaism*,
(Harvard, 1927), vol. i, p. 325.

[2] G. E. Phillips, *The Transmission of The Faith* (London, 1946), p. 54.

[3] *The Johannine Epistles* (London, 1946), commentary on 1. John 21,
p. 141.

[4] Acts 17. 16.   [5] Num. 21. 9.   [6] 2. Kings 18. 4.

Mount Sinai the dejected tribesmen, bereft of their leader Moses, who seemed lost on the mountain, made a golden calf. The people cried to Aaron, Moses' second-in-command, 'Make us gods which shall go before us; for as for this Moses, the man that brought us up out of the land of Egypt, we know not what is become of him.'[1] Aaron could only excuse himself later to Moses by pleading the pressure of the people and explaining how he had obtained golden ornaments from them, which he cast into the fire, 'and there came out this calf'[2] – as if it were an accident. Jeroboam I, however made no excuse for himself when he strengthened his position as king over Northern Israel, which had separated itself from the Southern Kingdom of Judah, by making 'two calves of gold: and he said unto them, It is too much for you to go up to Jerusalem: behold thy gods, O Israel, which brought thee up out of the land of Egypt. And he set the one in Bethel and the other in Dan.'[3]

The worship of Yahweh under the form of a bull or calf played a larger part in Israelite religion than the editors of the Old Testament books allowed. The condemnation of Jeroboam the son of Nebat that made Israel to sin derives from the editorial pen of a later age. In the eighth century B.C. Amos prophesied at Bethel. His stinging condemnation of social injustice caused him to be deported; but there is no record that he condemned the worship of Yahweh because it was associated with or directed through the image of a calf. This was condemned, however, by his younger contemporary, Hosea.[4] Gradually the position of the prophetic movement became clear. All physical representations of the deity were forbidden, even the simple pillars in the local shrines. The prophets attacked imported gods, which came in the trail of foreign princesses, and the native worship of the high places, which the Hebrews found in the land when

---

[1] Exod. 32. 1.   [2] Exod. 32. 24.   [3] 1. Kings 12. 28, 29.
[4] Hosea 8. 5, 6.

they invaded it, and which they took over with the arts of agriculture. Later historians assessed the righteousness or depravity of a king by his attitude to the high places, and, in the North, to the 'sin of the son of Nebat'. Under Josiah in the seventh century a considerable reformation took place, when an attempt was made to put into practice the requirements of Deuteronomy. But the great shock came with the Exile in Babylon (586–537 B.C.).

The leading members of the Kingdom of Judah were taken from their small country to what was then the greatest country in the world; from sparsely populated highlands to populous lowlands. Here many accepted the dominant commercial civilisation into which they were introduced: they became assimilated and were glad to stay. But for others the Exile was a calamitous punishment for national sin. It was not merely that they were separated from the land of their fathers; they felt exiled even from God.

> *By the rivers of Babylon,*
> *There we sat down, yea we wept*
> *When we remembered Zion. . . .*
> *How shall we sing the Lord's song*
> *In a strange land?*[1]

They learned, in time, that it was possible to do this very thing, and as a result of this process of education claimed the whole earth, the whole universe even, for the One they had known as the God of Israel. For the minority who were to set the tone for future Judaism the Exile was a punishment, a punishment inciting them to penitence. Their nation had been unfaithful: it must be faithful in the future. Laws had been broken: legislation must now be elaborated so that a loyal Jew should know exactly where he stood; should know exactly what the Law was and what would be the punishment for breaking it. Above all, the Exile was a

[1] Psalm 137. 1, 4.

judgment upon idolatry. There must be no idols in the future.

The Jews in exile did not only recall the folly of their nation's past infidelity and idolatry: they also recoiled in scornful horror from the idolatry of the rich and powerful people by whom they had been taken captive. The tremendous images whose sight was inescapable as they threaded their way through the crowded streets of the world's capital city did not impress them as magnificent but as horrible, as ludicrous even. The sound of ironic laughter rises from the pages of Isaiah 44, as the prophet describes how men set about making themselves gods of wood:

'. . . a man will fix upon some plane or oak, which God planted and the rain nourished to serve as fuel; men kindle a fire with it to warm themselves, they start a blaze in order to bake bread. But he turns it into a god for worship; he makes it into an idol and bows down to it! Half of it he burns in the fire, roasting flesh upon the embers; he eats the roast meant and is satisfied, warming himself and saying, "Ha, I am warm now, I feel the glow!" The other half he turns into a god, into an idol, and bows down to it, worshipping it, praying to it, crying "Save me, for thou art my god!" Such men are ignorant and senseless, their eyes are bedaubed till they cannot see, and their minds closed to knowledge; none of them calls to mind – and has sense and wit enough to say to himself, "Half of it I burned in the fire, baking bread upon its embers and roasting meat for food; and am I to make the other half a horrid idol? Am I to bow down to a wooden image?"[1]

As Judaism developed in the restored community in Jerusalem and its immediate vicinity, after a small proportion of the exiles had returned, the rejection of images was carried to fantastic lengths, which were only possible, as

[1] Isaiah 44. 14–19. tr. James Moffatt.

Bertholet has suggested, among a people whose sense for plastic art was undeveloped. 'It speaks volumes that the Hebrews had one and the same word for to "paint" and to "smear", or to "anoint".[1] The Jews were hard put to it to maintain their imageless worship in a world of idolatry. Paul was amazed by the number of idols in Athens; but there must have been plenty in Tarsus, as in the cities of Decapolis, very near to the Lake of Galilee, in the days of our Lord. Herod the Great, who expressed a cynical temper in the great works he undertook, not only rebuilt the Temple with great magnificence, but erected in near-by Samaria, re-named Sebaste, a great temple to the Emperor Augustus.[2] His new seaport, Caesarea, was also predominantly a heathen and therefore idolatrous city. Jewish purists reacted from the pressure of this environment by such declarations as that a statue used for idolatrous purposes was not only to be pulverised, but the dust cast to the winds or into the sea, lest it might possibly serve as manure to the soil.[3] Jewish controversial writings of the Hellenistic period were also full of arguments against idolatry. The reader with an Apocrypha in his Bible will find a good example of this in the Wisdom of Solomon, chapters 13 to 15.

In 63 B.C. the Roman general Gnæus Pompeius Magnus – commonly known as Pompey – having captured Jerusalem, entered the Temple with a group of officers, and penetrate to the Holy of Holies. They were looking for an idol. But to their astonishment they found none. This must have seemed to them evidence of madness just as much as did the idolatry of Babylon to the prophet of the Exile. Later the Jews persuaded the Roman procurators to leave their standards outside the city, because they had images on them. Pontius

[1] *A History of Hebrew Civilization* (London, 1928), p. 306.

[2] Cf. Moore, *Judaism*, vol. i. p. 363.

[3] A. Edersheim, *The Life and Times of Jesus the Messiah* (London, 1906), vol. ii, p. 666.

Pilate, however, was determined not to be thwarted by what he considered superstition. He allowed the standards to be brought in by night; and at once the city was in an uproar. ' As soon as they knew it, they came in multitudes to Caesarea and interceded with Pilate many days, that he would remove the images; and when he would not grant their requests, because it would tend to the injury of Caesar, while yet they persevered in their request, on the sixth day he ordered his soldiers to have their weapons privately, while he came and sat upon his judgment-seat, which seat was so prepared in the open place of the city, that it concealed the army that lay ready to oppress them; and when the Jews petitioned him again, he gave a signal to the soldiers to encompass them round, and threatened that their punishment should not be less than immediate death, unless they would leave off disturbing him, and go their ways home. But they threw themselves upon the ground, and laid their necks bare, and said they would take their deaths very willingly, rather than the wisdom of their laws should be transgressed.' This sit-down strike was effective, for Josephus records that ' Pilate was deeply affected with their firm resolution to keep their laws inviolable, and presently commanded the images to be carried back from Jerusalem to Caesarea.'[1]

It was obviously no use expecting these Jews to behave in normal fashion. There was a streak of fanaticism about them which could not be evaded. 'Of all figures in the old Mediterranean world, the strangest and most enigmatic alike to his fellow-subjects and to the modern student of history is the Jew.'[2] What made first-century Jews enigmatic to their contemporaries in the Roman Empire were their food-laws, their Sabbath, their exclusiveness, and, above all, their strange, image-less worship. In different ways the Christian

[1] *Antiquities* XVIII, iii, 1.

[2] T. R. Glover, *The World of the New Testament* (Cambridge, 1931), p. 88.

Church was in each of these matters an inheritor of Judaism; and to their contemporaries, if not to the modern student of history, the early Christians appeared equally enigmatic. They also did not use images. The second-century opponent of Christianity, Celsus, states that Christians 'could not tolerate either temples, altars or images'; and Origen replies that it is on the ground of the Second Commandment that Christians abhor all worship or use of images, and adds, 'It is not possible at the same time to know God and to address prayers to images.' The use of the crucifix in Christian worship appears to have been unknown until the sixth century.[1] To many people in the early centuries Christians seemed to be a new kind of Jews. Nor is it altogether surprising that believers in the God and Father of our Lord Jesus Christ were often called atheists.

The Christians' rejection of idolatry involved them in a social isolation which many Gentile converts must have found hard to bear. The problem arose particularly in Corinth. This was a city with an evil reputation. On the stage a native of Corinth was usually represented drunk.[2] It was a city of pleasure where immorality was a part of the idolatrous worship of Aphrodite; a cosmopolitan city of 600,000 inhabitants drawn from many parts of the world. It is well for us to recall this background when we consider the weakness of the Corinthian Church and reflect that it was to the Church in this city that St. Paul sent the matchless Hymn to the divine love which we know as 1. Corinthians 13.

The Church in Corinth was, of course, a tiny minority. It could not be expected to provide its own butchers – as did the larger Jewish community. But if one bought meat in the market it had probably been first offered up in an idol temple. What was a busy housewife to do? After all, a Christian knew

[1] See R. H. Charles, *The Decalogue* (Second Edition, Edinburgh, 1926), pp. 38, 42, 43.

[2] H. L. Goudge, *The First Epistle to the Corinthians* (Third Edition, London, 1911), p. xv.

that the god represented by the idol simply did not exist: there was only one God, maker of Heaven and Earth. And what about going out to parties? 'When the hunting club of the Artemisians held a banquet, for example, they began by sacrificing part of the meat to Artemis, their patron deity. Or a private party might be given, nominally as a "table of the lord Serapis", the proceedings being opened by a similar sacrifice. It was all part and parcel of the formal etiquette in society. Were Christian churchmen to cut themselves off from these entertainments, in a nervous, sour spirit? If idols meant nothing to them, if they made no secret of their utter indifference to the traditional religious setting, and if no pagan friend objected, why raise scruples and give way to fads?'[1] This was the argument of one section in the Corinthian Church. But there were others who were appalled by the very idea of eating what had been consecrated to an idol. What was a Christian to do?

It was in relation to this question that St. Paul made the famous saying, 'All things are lawful but all things are not expedient.' He saw the force of the argument outlined above. He agreed that an idol was nothing. Yet, at the same time, he recognised that to allow a complete freedom in this matter would be unsettling to those who were not strong in the faith. He therefore set out a compromise. So far as marketing was concerned the Christian housewife was to ask no unnecessary questions: for the earth is the Lord's and the fulness thereof. When invited out to dinner a Christian was similarly to eat what was put in front of him, without asking questions. But if the host should say, 'This has been offered in sacrifice,' the Christian was to leave that dish alone. Nothing had really happened to the meat; for the idol was nothing. But there might be some Christian with a lingering suspicion that the idol was, after all, something: it was for his sake, and so

[1] James Moffatt, *The First Epistle of Paul to the Corinthians*, (London, 1938), p. 102.

that there might be no possible misunderstanding by the non-Christian host, that the guest was to refrain.[1] Here was being enunciated a principle which reaches back to the Old Testament, but which receives its classic expression in that hymn to charity which St. Paul included in the same Epistle, that of consideration for weaker brothers. Paul had learned from his Master that the danger most of all to be avoided was that of causing others to stumble. And from his discussion of this practical issue before the Church there emerged one of the greatest of New Testament phrases: 'For if a man see thee which hast knowledge sitting at meat in an idol's temple, will not his conscience, if he is weak, be emboldened to eat things sacrificed to idols? For through thy knowledge he that is weak perisheth, the brother for whose sake Christ died.'[1]

The same arguments which had currency in the Corinthian Church were later used in favour of not making too much fuss about sacrificing to the genius of Emperor. After all it was a matter of etiquette. No one who had had contact with Roman Emperors was likely to take his divinity very seriously. Why not do what was required and save bother? Moreover it was a necessary act to clear the suspicion of disloyalty. But for a Christian to take part in an act of worship in which he did not believe was to debase all true worship; to use meaningless words was to undermine the meaning of all words. How could he turn from the cynical worship of the Emperor to the devoted worship of God revealed in Christ?

This is how a modern historian of the Romans puts it:

'The Christian refused; the state persisted; each misunderstood the other; each started from an opposite point. To the Roman the unity of the Empire was of vital importance, and homage to 'Rome and Augustus" embodied and expressed that ideal. It was an act of political faith. Other cults were perfectly prepared to render that homage – except

[1] 1. Cor. 10. 25–29.   [1] 1. Cor. 8, 10, 11.

the Jews, with whom as a race the Government had come to terms; but such terms could not be granted to Christians who claimed converts in every race. Besides, the Jews did render annual sacrifice in the Temple on behalf of the Emperor, and that was enough. To the Christian the act of homage to the divinity – whatever that might mean – of Rome and Augustus was an act of religious faith, and inconsistent with the Christian faith. Hence arose the misunderstanding; neither side could see the other's point of view. Moreover, there were Christians who felt that every daily act which contributed to the welfare of the state contributed to the maintenance of idolatry. Thus, one side thought in political terms, the other in religious terms; and, as the religion was quite unlike any other in its refusal to "live and let live", conflict was inevitable. The Christian claim to universalism seemed to aim at a state within the state, spreading its propaganda in secret. The Roman point of view is entirely intelligible.'[1]

In time, however, the Roman Empire was obliged to come to terms with the growing Church. When, in the fourth century, Christianity became the official religion of the Roman Empire the Church had also come to terms with the world. From this time onwards the endeavour to maintain worship without images was only partially successful. Nor, indeed, was the strict Jewish abhorrence of pictorial art there from the beginning. Quite early in the Roman catacombs, there were illustrations of the miracles of Jesus, of Jesus as the Good Shepherd, of Daniel in the lions' den, as well as many Christian symbols. But these were hardly objects of veneration; they were not worshipped. With the wholesale turning to Christianity which followed the conversion of Constantine, in many a village the local saint took the place of the local god, and was given honour in the god's old shrine. Among ignorant people a growth of superstition

[1] R. H. Barrow, *The Romans* (London, 1949), p. 182.

was inevitable, the veneration not only of the saint's relics, but of the saint's statue as if it were itself a god. The reverence accorded to the Virgin Mary by ignorant peasants in Catholic countries must often strike many non-Catholics as idolatrous.

There were protests. In the eighth century the simple faith of the Emperor Leo, who had been stung by the taunt of idolatry flung at Christians by Mohammedans, took measures which initiated the Iconoclastic – or image-breaking – controversy. This policy 'had both its religious and social sides, and was destined to rend the internal harmony of the Empire. But it also arrested a dangerous disease. . . . Supersitition and the belief in the marvellous had grown till men neglected their own exertions and left all to the interposition of the saints and the Virgin Mother of God. Above all, the cult offered to miracle-working images filled an enormous place in Byzantine minds. Everywhere the sacred icons (likenesses) were adored and besought for every desire. They were even made godparents at baptism. Theologians declared that it was the mystical presence of the saint in his icon which was invoked, but the populace drew no such distinction.'[1]

The Reformation brought a far greater iconoclastic assault. Hammers and pickaxes were brought into churches to break up statuary which to-day would be considered priceless. An Anglican cannot but regret the beauty which was so ruthlessly destroyed in so many of the churches we have inherited. But it was not pointless destruction. Latimer had the image of the Virgin in Worcester Cathedral, 'our great Sibyll', as he called it, stripped of its jewels and eventually burned in London. 'She herself with her old sister of Walsingham, her young sister of Ipswich, with their two other sisters of Doncaster and Penrice would make a

[1] C. W. Previté-Orton, *The Shorter Cambridge Medieval History* (Cambridge, 1953), vol. i, p. 247.

jolly muster in Smithfield.'[1] The words are coarse and seem shocking. But those who are shocked by them might well ask themselves what authority they give to the Second Commandment.

The Council which met at Nicaea in 787 and which restored the cult of images after they had been forbidden by iconoclastic Emperors distinguished between the veneration (*proskunesis*) which might be offered to them, and the adoration (*latreia*) which might be offered only to God. This is not a distinction which in practice it is easy to maintain. 'It is idolatry', says Bishop Gore, 'to let our worship (1) be directed towards persons lower than God, as mediators, because they seem easier to approach and less awful; or (2) rest upon circumscribed objects so as to imperil the omnipresence of God; or (3) be moulded by false conceptions of God, as when the worth of prayer is estimated by the place where it is offered, or by some measure of length.'[2] The Church, in all its divisions, has probably failed in all these ways. Better not to be censorious, but to reflect, if it be possible, the wide charity of Sir Thomas Browne, 'At the sight of a Cross or Crucifix I can dispense with my hat, but scarce with the thought or memory of my Saviour . . . I could never hear the Ave-Mary Bell without an elevation; or think it a sufficient warrant, because *they* erred in one circumstance, for me to err in all, that is, in silence and dumb contempt. Whilst, therefore, they directed their Devotions to *Her*, I offered mine to God, and rectified the Errors of their Prayers by rightly ordering mine own.'[3]

Pitfalls abound in all true worship; and the temptations of the godly are more subtle and more grievous than those of the ungodly. It is easy to retreat into a puritanism which

[1] *Dictionary of English Church History* (Third Edition, London, 1948), p. 323.

[2] *The Sermon on the Mount* (London, 1896), p. 208.

[3] *Religio Medici* (Temple Classics Edition, London, 1896), p. 4.

treats all human possessions and delights as the enslavement of sin; to do this in reaction from the temper which cries *Carpe diem*, 'Gather ye rosebuds while ye may.' 'Take thine ease, eat, drink and be merry.' Between the extremes of puritanism and sensualism there lies a sacramentalism which can discern behind the creation the Creator, which would consecrate the best of human gifts to the service of the Giver, which can discern on all hands and in all places outward and visible signs of an inward and spiritual grace. The pictured walls and windows of medieval churches have long been defended as the lesson-books of the unlearned: nor do great Gothic cathedrals, for all their multiplicity of carving, suggest idolatry. They bring the worshipper to his knees in adoration of the One whom the heaven of heavens cannot contain. It is a great tradition that only the best should be used for God's glory, the best materials, the most skilful workmanship. And shall we deny to the sculptor that exercise of his craft which is his prayer, so that in the houses of God there shall be wrought from stone neither mounting angels nor praying saints, nor even the Virgin bent over her Child? The tension is inescapable between the feelings of the artist and the demands of intellectual truth; yet all these things can rightly be used where their presence is not that of overloaded ornament, extravagant and insincere, but a genuine aid to the worship of the Almighty. The danger comes not from a great array of statuary but from the individual shrine, where it is easy to lapse into the idolatry of worship which 'rests upon circumscribed objects so as to imperil the omnipresence of God.' This may have been felt by the English reformers, whose first harsh attacks were upon chantry chapels.

There is a danger of idolatry within Christianity: there is danger of idolatry outside; an idolatry practised by modern, emancipated men, who feel that they are free from religion altogether. When totalitarian governments first arose in recent years much was written to show that here was a new type of idolatry, enslaving great masses of people, evoking in the most ardent devotees a hysteria which was half-brother to insanity. Democratic peoples have reprobated the idolatry of state and of class, while they have hardly been aware that they have been caught up in idolatries of their own. 'Thus saith the Lord,' declared Jeremiah, 'Cursed is the man that trusteth in man, and maketh flesh his arm, and whose heart departeth from the Lord. For he shall be like the heath in the desert, and shall not see when good cometh; but shall inhabit the parched places in the wilderness, a salt land and not inhabited.'[1] The generation of the great trusters in humanity has mostly been disillusioned. We have few men to-day like the Abbé Siéyès to utter a belief in man's infinite perfectibility. We do not trust in man; but we trust in what man has made. Idol follows idol into the temple of twentieth-century popularity. At one moment we cry to Science, 'Save me, for thou art my god!' and at another the cry is to Education. The setting up of the United Nations, the achievement of the welfare state, the employment of atomic energy for industrial purposes, above all, perhaps, our standard of living, each of these seems for a short time to be means by which a wholesome society, and perhaps a wholesome world, is to be attained. But the only wholesome society is one in which the holy has its right place. These things fail because too much is expected of them. Not one of them can reach the root of the disease, which is in the nature of man himself. His need is to be mastered by One greater than himself, in whose service alone he shall find true freedom.

A conviction behind this book is that disobedience to all and every one of the Commandments de-personalises man and his society; making them less than the man and the society they were intended to be. This is clearly true of

[1] Jer. 17. 5, 6.

idolatry, whether it be a bowing down to gods of wood and stone, or abasement before any human artefacts, or the infantilism implicit in the use of mascots and charms. In giving himself to what is less than man he becomes less than man. Yet the constant irruption of idolatry into human society from the earliest to the present age points to a basic need of man. The need is that God should not be merely distant, immortal, invisible, and, if one might so put it, unsociable. Man needs both the distant God and the near God; and both needs are met, a Christian believes, by the incarnation of God in Christ. The far God has become the near God; has revealed, in fact, that He was the near God all the time. Jesus has become the window through which we look to God. He is, says St. Paul, the image, the *eikon*, of the invisible God.[1] And the effect of Christian preaching has been a leap from littleness to greatness – a greatness which transfigures all little things. 'Ye turned to God from idols, to serve the living and true God,'[2] St. Paul reminded his converts in Thessalonica. And when at Lystra the two apostles, Barnabas and Paul, suddenly found themselves being accorded divine honours, they cried out in horror and entreaty, 'Sirs, why do ye these things? We also are men of like passions with you, and bring you good tidings, that ye should turn from these vain things unto the living God.'[3] That remains the good tidings of Christianity; a message to those outside, who too easily spend their lives in the pursuit of vanities; but a message to Christians also, to cast out idols from their hearts.

What are we to make of the conception of a jealous god? Is it something outgrown, to be rejected like the attribution of divine vengeance, when children mocked the prophet Elisha, and forty-two of them were ravaged by two she-bears out of the wood?[4] Is the divine jealousy something

[1] Col. 1. 15.   [2] 1. Thess. 1. 9.   [3] Acts 14. 15, 16.
[4] 2. Kings 2. 24.

which comes under the heading *Ye have heard that it was said by them of old time . . . but I say unto you!*

The New Testament would not agree entirely with this modern watering down. The New Testament has much to say about the judgment of God, about 'the goodness and severity of God.'[1] For the New Testament God is a Father, the Father even of the prodigal son, but this does not make Him an indulgent, twentieth-century parent, who does not know what it is to punish. What we may well question is the attribution to God of the human emotion of anger. Professor Dodd concludes a remarkable discussion of the wrath of God with these words: 'It is to be noted . . . there is something impersonal about "the Wrath of God" from the beginning, and something incapable of being wholly personalized in the development of religious ideas. It is only to a God not yet fully conceived in terms of moral personality that the primitive numinous terror can be directed. The idea of an angry God is a first attempt to rationalize the shuddering awe which men felt before the incalculable possibilities of appalling disaster inherent in life, but it is an attempt which breaks down as the rational element in religion advances. In the long run we cannot think with full consistency of God in terms of the highest human ideals of personality and yet attribute to Him the irrational passion of anger.'[2]

This may help us to understand the picture of both punishment and mercy extending over the generations. It is a severe sentence; affecting grandchildren and great-grandchildren; but we know that it is true to life. Every age suffers from the mistakes of its immediate past; and there are families where the inheritance is tragically worked out. But it is not for us to consider the 'if onlys' of yesterday: we must face the 'if onlys' of to-day; for it is here and now that

[1] Rom. 11. 22.

[2] *The Epistle of Paul to the Romans* (Moffatt N. T. Commentaries. London, 1932), p. 24.

we have a responsibility, not only to our contemporaries, but to those who shall come after us.

The jealous God is jealous for His good name; for the maintenance of His covenant; for an understanding of His character among men. This is an experience which His servants can reflect and share; sometimes to a point of human pride, where they become almost sorry for their Maker. So Elijah said, 'I have been very jealous for the Lord, the God of hosts; for the children of Israel have forsaken thy covenant, thrown down thine altars, and slain thy prophets with the sword: and I, even I only am left; and they seek my life to take it away.'[1] Elijah needed to be told that God was quite capable of taking care of Himself – a reminder still required by some despairing congregations.

The prophets in Hebrew history were not only enthusiasts for God: they were witnesses to the enthusiasm of God. He is a God who achieves His ends despite all obstacles. He is not to be trifled with or set at naught. There is a fear of the Lord which is an essential beginning of any human wisdom. Jesus took on where the prophets left off. In Him we see the jealous God – or shall we not say, with Martin Buber, the *zealous* God? – going to all lengths to win men's love; going to the lengths even of rejection and death upon a cross. 'That a good man may have his back to the wall is no more than we knew already; but that God could have his back to the wall is a boast for all insurgents for ever. Christianity is the only religion on earth that has felt that omnipotence made God incomplete. Christianity alone has felt that God, to be wholly God, must have been a rebel as well as a king. Alone of all creeds, Christianity has added courage to the virtues of the Creator.'[2]

God's jealousy is revealed to Christians as His questing love; the love that will not be denied; the love which,

[1] 2. Kings 19. 10.

[2] G. K. Chesterton, *Orthodoxy* (London, 1908), p. 254.

because it is compacted of sacrifice, is not to be trifled with. It is the chivalry of Him who was in all points tempted like as we are, yet without sin; who said 'I have not called you servants, but I have called your friends'; who said, 'Greater love hath no man than this that a man lay down his life for his friends'; but went beyond His word and died for His enemies.

III

GOD'S NAME IN VAIN

Thou shalt not take the name of the Lord thy God in vain; for the Lord will not hold him guiltless that taketh his name in vain. *Exodus. 20. 7.*

Ye shall not swear by my name falsely, so that thou profane the name of thy God. I am the Lord. *Leviticus 19. 12.*

The Lord is great in Sion: and high above all people. They shall give thanks unto thy Name: which is great, wonderful, and holy. *Psalm 99. 3.*

He sent redemption unto his people: he hath commanded his covenant for ever; holy and reverend is his name.
Psalm 111. 9.

Thou, O Lord, art in the midst of us, and we are called by thy name: leave us not. *Jeremiah 14. 9.*

For the scripture saith Whosoever believeth on him shall not be put to shame. For there is no distinction between Jew and Greek: for the same Lord is Lord of all, and is rich unto all that call upon him: for whosoever shall call upon the name of the Lord shall be saved. *Romans 10. 11–13.*

Where two or three are gathered together in my name, there am I in the midst of them. *Matthew 18. 20.*

Lord of all power and might, who art the author and giver of all good things; Graft in our hearts the love of thy Name, increase in us true religion, nourish us with all goodness, and of thy great mercy keep us in the same; through Jesus Christ our Lord. Amen.

Collect for the seventh Sunday after Trinity.

———————

I T IS a fundamental belief, both of Christianity and Judaism, not only that God created the universe and man, but that He made man 'in his own image.' This means that man's nature has been made so that it can respond to God; that fellowship between Creator and created is not only possible but is intended; that only in that fellowship does man attain the fulness of his being. Yet, as God is a free agent, so must one made in His image be. Fellowship can be neither automatic nor constrained; it must be freely offered. God invites, offers, entreats: He stands at the door and knocks: He does not force His way in.

The whole of human history may be seen as a response – or a failure to respond – to the gracious love of God. Disaster came early. The myth of the Fall dramatises an inescapable human experience:

> *Video meliora, proboque :*
> *Deteriora sequor.*[1]

wrote Ovid, anticipating by a generation the cry of St. Paul, 'O wretched man that I am! who shall deliver me out of the body of this death?'[2] Theologians have argued whether the image of God in man be totally effaced or marred only. Those who take the former position may be hard put to it to explain not so much the problem of evil as the problem of good; the fellowship with God which *has* been experienced

[1] *Metamorphoses* vii, 20, "I see and approve better things, but follow worse."

[2] Rom. 7. 24.

in every generation, and which is one of the most forceful arguments for man's continued belief in God. 'There is a living God,' said Archbishop Söderblom on his death-bed, 'I can prove it by the history of religions.' Here, at any rate, is evidence not lightly to be put on one side. Tennyson's affirmation, 'We needs must love the highest when we see it'[1] is not, alas, wholly validated by human experience. But some men do love the highest; while many others feel that they ought to do so. Here is a claim which they recognise but dare not admit. Man's true nature finds its fulfilment only in response to God. But the image of God has been so defaced in man that he is for ever denying his nature.

What matters is relationship; relationship between God and man, and the consequent relationship between man and man; relationship with a God who is increasingly apprehended as personal, in the doing of whose will men themselves become personal; relationship with a God who has Himself taken the initiative to make that relationship possible. With this great theme the whole of theology is concerned; consequent upon it, for the Christian as for the Jew, is the whole of ethics.

Already we have considered two barriers to relationship created by man. The first was belief in many gods. For the polytheist the god whom at any moment he is worshipping or endeavouring in his daily living to obey, is but one among many. It is hard for him to give to this particular god complete trust; for there may be another god, more powerful or more subtle, able to thwart his will. Once the polytheist begins to doubt the ability of other gods the way to monotheism has been charted. He will soon be doubting their existence. As Dr. W. R. Matthews has put it, 'There is an inner logic or dialectic which pushes the religious consciousness beyond the polytheistic stage . . . When once the human spirit has, however simply, come to recognise the

[1] *Idylls of the King. Guinevere*, i. 655.

more than natural necessities of its life the knell of poly-theism has sounded. The many gods can give no ground for the apprehension of the world as an intelligible system, while the many divine wills, often in antagonism, of the best ordered pantheon can furnish no adequate response to a moral outlook which has apprehended the universal char-acter of moral good.'[1] God is not only the Creator: He is ever seeking out those whom He has made, endeavouring to win them to Himself, to overcome the barriers to relationships which they have made.

The second barrier to relationship is idolatry; which causes men, in their aspiration towards God, to halt at some image or human creation, so that, in St. Paul's words, they 'worshipped and served the creature rather than the Creator.'[2] Idolatry is usually associated with polytheism, with the heathen in his blindness bowing down to wood and stone; but it is the temptation of many in the modern age, who put their trust in human contrivances rather than in God. They may believe in God, but there is no reality of fellowship. They take Him for granted – as many a partner does in many a marriage – turning to Him with real feeling only in times of danger or crisis.

Taking God's name in vain has its basis in legal usage; and its primary meaning is perjury. From the earliest days of human intercourse statements have been giving an addi-tional and more emphatic guarantee of genuineness by making them in the presence of God, by inviting, indeed, the punishment of God should the statement prove false, or should the man who makes it fail to perform what he has promised. There is a familiar illustration in the moving speech of Ruth to Naomi: 'Intreat me not to leave thee, and to return from following after thee: for whither thou goest, I will go; and where thou lodgest I will lodge: thy people

[1] *God in Christian Thought and Experience* (London, 1930), p. 37.
[2] Rom. 1. 25.

shall be my people, and thy God my God: where thou diest, will I die, and there will I be buried: *the Lord do so to me, and more also*, if aught but death part thee and me.'[1] In a world of uncertainty and deceit it has not been thought sufficient for yea to be yea and nay nay.

The way in which oaths originated may be deduced from a passage in Exodus:

'If a man deliver unto his neighbour an ass, or an ox, or a sheep, or any beast, to keep; and it die, or be hurt, or drive away, no man seeing it: the oath of the Lord shall be between them both, whether he hath put his hand unto his neighbour's goods; and the owner thereof shall accept it, and he shall not make restitution.'[2]

The essential point here is in the words *no man seeing it*. No witness is available. If the man in charge of the beast is ready to swear to the truth of his statement, that is to be accepted, and there is to be no further inquiry.

An oath originated as a conditional curse, called down by a man upon himself, inviting the punishment of God, if a statement be not true or a promise not kept. This sense of the invitation of punishment is not in great evidence to-day; but oaths are still used as a solemn appeal to God in witness to the truth of a statement. It still serves this purpose in English law-courts, in undertakings entered into before a Commissioner for Oaths, and when a petitioner for a licence to be married swears to the truth of an affidavit solemnly made in the presence of a Surrogate. The nineteenth chapter of Leviticus contains many essentials for healthy social living. At its heart is the statement, 'Ye shall not swear by my name falsely'[3] – for when that happens healthy social living is no

[1] Ruth 1. 16, 17. Cf. 1. Sam. 20. 13, 25. 22. 1. Kings 2. 23.

[2] Exod. 22. 10, 11.

[3] Lev. 19. 12.

longer possible. Where there cannot be trust there can only be a restrained form of anarchy.

When that condition exists between nations it is nowadays called the cold war. It is this sense of anarchy barely restrained which allows the editor of a newspaper to write that 'in international affairs there is, in the ultimate, no moral conscience.'[1] That could hardly be said so long as even lip-service was paid to the myth of a Christendom uniting the nations in a family under God. It has not made for international good relations that the sense of 'the Lord do so to me and more also' has passed from engagements solemnly entered into, which are often lightly set aside as policy or profit may dictate. After the First World War there was a sense of relief in the determination to get away from the old secret diplomacy and to enter a new era of open diplomacy. But the new era presented new temptations to infidelity. There is an openness, as Sir Harold Nicolson has pointed out, which 'leads to imprecision, No statesman is prepared in advance and in the open to bind himself to a precise policy. An imprecise policy means no policy at all.'[2] The modern negotiator in foreign affairs must always be wondering what the voters will think, whether what he is doing will go down well; or whether it can be presented so as to go down well. There is the danger also of saying pleasant things, so as to avoid the unpleasant duty of saying unpleasant things. All tends to breed irresponsibility; and irresponsibility produces cynicism. The ultimate responsibility in public affairs, as in private affairs, is a responsibility to God. And God is the God of truth.

In more limited spheres there is a danger even among those who treat legal oaths with proper seriousness, the danger of treating God as a mere convenience. A Commissioner for Oaths is commonly regarded as performing a solemn duty:

[1] See p. 13.

[2] *Peacemaking 1919* (London, 1933), p. 208.

it is not often regarded as a holy one. Yet, day by day to be calling upon men and women to swear by Almighty God is, if it mean anything at all, to be reminding them that there is a Power supreme over the universe to whom they are answerable. But it becomes ill a minister of religion to be self-righteous in such a matter. He knows that to no other person is the temptation so frequent to take God's name in vain; to make Him a convenience; to forget the divine reality in a welter of human words.

A Christian has to take seriously the words of Jesus in the Sermon on the Mount: 'Again ye have heard that it was said to them of old time, Thou shalt not forswear thyself, but shalt perform unto the Lord thine oaths: but I say unto you, Swear not at all: neither by heaven, for it is the throne of God; nor by the earth, for it is the footstool of his feet; nor by Jerusalem, for it is the city of the great king. Neither shalt thou swear by thy head, for thou canst not make one hair white or black. But let your speech be, Yea, Yea; Nay, Nay: and whatsoever more is of the evil one.'[1] On the face of it, this seems to forbid any taking of oaths at all; and so it has been interpreted by some of the early Fathers of the Church, and by the Society of Friends. Yet the interpretation of Christ's teaching needs to be checked by His own practice; and this suggests that He was attacking looseness of speech rather than the formal use of an oath in a legal ceremony. Jesus Himself took the judicial oath when it was put to Him in its most solemn form by the High Priest at His trial: 'I adjure thee by the living God.'[2] St. Paul also would use such phrases as 'God is my witness,'[3] 'behold, before God, I lie not,'[4] 'I call God for a witness upon my soul.'[5] It was common among the Jews of our Lord's time, as it is common among many people to-day, to use the name of God to add strength to a statement in ordinary conversation. This Jesus

[1] Matt. 5. 33–37.   [2] Matt. 26. 63.   [3] Phil. 1. 8.
[4] Gal. 1. 20.   [5] 2. Cor. 1. 20.

forbids. If the statement be untrue there is a direct insult to God: but if it be true it may also be irreverent; for it is a dragging of God down to the human level. It is an example of the familiarity which breeds contempt. Also forbidden by Jesus are 'the casuistical distinctions which the Rabbis drew between the different degrees of oaths, the hollowness of which our Lord exposes, on the ground that as soon as the words "I swear" have been uttered a sacred engagement is contracted which involves God whether His name is actually invoked or not.'[1]

Reverence, in our day, is becoming a neglected factor in life; and it is something without which a people perishes. There was a good deal to be said in favour of the biographers of the twenties of this century who began the fashion of "de-bunking' heroes. Some of the figures of the nineteenth century, whom the young had been taught to admire, had not been, perhaps, so very heroic. But heroes existed then, as they do to-day; and there is nothing to be said for the fashion of treating all men as impostors. As reverence for God has diminished so has reverence for man; for how shall their fellows regard with reverence those made in the image of a Creator about whom they are flippant? 'You must discover in all these men and women,' said Bishop Phillips Brooks in his *Lectures on Preaching*, 'some inherent preciousness for which even the marvel of the Incarnation and the agony of Calvary was not too great'[2] – but how shall there be preciousness in man if man's Maker be treated with contempt? And that, essentially, is what it means to take God's name in vain. Man was made for communion with God, more than that, for the vision of God. To deny that possibility is to degrade man from his dignity. 'The lamp of the body is the eye: if therefore thine eye be single they whole body shall be full of light. But if thine eye be evil thy whole

[1] F. W. Green, *Saint Matthew* (Clarendon Bible, Oxford, 1936), p. 134.
[2] *Lectures on Preaching* (London 1895), p. 260.

body shall be full of darkness, If therefore the light that is in thee be darkness, how great is that darkness.'[1]

It is a strange fact that the less people believe in God the more ready they seem to use His name and the name of Jesus Christ in their daily speech. Whereas churchgoers are often too shy of speaking God's name – perhaps from a Jewish inheritance which we shall consider in a moment – non-churchgoers are often not shy at all. The thoughtless oaths by which the speech of some is punctuated may be a form of rebellion against a domination from which they think they have escaped, but are not quite sure. Leaving, however, these mysteries of the unconscious to the psychologists, we must note that there is something here against which a Christian must be on his guard. Few things are more contagious than fashions of speech. It is for a Christian to remember that the God whom others treat lightly is for Him the greatest of all realities, that the Christ whose name is uttered in derision is the One who has brought life and immortality to light.

The name of God meant much to the Hebrews. It was so holy that though it was often written it was never spoken. When a reader in the Jewish synagogue came to the sacred letters JHVH he substituted for them the word *Adonay*, meaning *The Lord*. Hebrew writing, like modern shorthand, was composed of consonants only. The vowels were later supplied, for those who might be uncertain of oral tradition, by a series of small marks, called vowel points, above, around, and below the consonantal text, but never interfering with it. Thus around the letters of the name of God there were supplied the vowels of the word *Adonay*, which was to be read; and as a result, in comparatively modern times the hybrid word Jehovah made its appearance, composed of the sacred name JHVH and the vowels of Adonay. Wherever the words 'the Lord' appear in the English

[1] Matt. 6. 22, 23.

versions of the Old Testament, the sacred name JHVH is to
be presumed in the original. How it was actually pronounced
we are not sure. Modern scholars write it Jahveh or Yahweh.
But it must rarely have been pronounced at all. Even in
writing it a scribe had to be most cautious. The copyist of the
Law must sit in full Jewish dress, be newly bathed, and never
dip his pen in ink in the middle of writing the name of God;
indeed, should a king address him while writing that
name he must take no notice of him. If regulations could
prevent men taking God's name in vain, prevented it
would be.

All this was done because the name of God was more than
a mark on vellum or a sound breathed into the air. God's
name meant God's presence. ('Where two or three are
gathered together in my name,' said Jesus also, 'there am
I in the midst of them,')[1] The sanctuary of God was the place
where He chose to cause His name to dwell.[2] To use God's
name was therefore to invite His presence. To do this flip-
pantly or irreverently was to insult the Almighty. *Holy is his
name*, the phrase in the *Magnificat* has an extensive Old
Testament background. 'They shall give thanks unto thy
name: which is great, wonderful, and holy,' we read in the
Psalms. The phrase, also, 'the name of God,' was used from
a fear of the use of the bare name, God. The root idea of
'holy' as we find it in the Old Testament is that of separation. God's name is holy, because 'my thoughts are not your
thoughts, neither are your ways my ways, saith the Lord.
For as the heavens are higher than the earth so are my ways
higher than your ways, and my thoughts than your thoughts.'[3]
But by God Himself that separation is being continually
overcome; and it is significant that the passage just quoted is
introduced by an appeal for men to return to God, who is
willing to welcome the penitent. 'Let the wicked forsake his

[1] Matt. 18. 20.   [2] Deut. 12. 11, 16. 2, 26. 2.
[3] Isaiah 55. 8, 9.

way and the unrighteous man his thoughts: and let him return unto the Lord, and he will have mercy upon him; and to our God, for he will abundantly pardon.'[1] Across the separation of man's sin comes the gracious invitation. 'For thus saith the high and lofty one that inhabiteth eternity, whose name is Holy. I dwell in the high and holy place, with him also that is of a contrite and humble spirit, to revive the spirit of the humble and to revive the heart of the contrite ones.'[2]

Christianity goes even further. The New Testament record is of God Himself coming from the other side of the separation to save mankind. The human name of the One who carried through the great act is Jesus, or Saviour. 'Thou shalt call his name Jesus; for it is he that shall save his people from their sins.'[3] Nor is this all. St. Paul was bold enough to declare that to Jesus, crucified for man's sin, there was given the unutterable name of God Himself. For this is the meaning of the conclusion of the great hymn of praise in Philippians: 'Wherefore also God highly exalted him, and gave unto him the name which is above every name; that in the name of Jesus every knee should bow, of things in heaven, and things on earth and things under the earth, and that every tongue should confess that *Jesus Christ is Lord*, to the glory of God the Father.'[4] Here the name referred to is not, as a casual reading might suggest, the name Jesus but the name *of* Jesus, the name given to Jesus; and that name is Lord, the Greek *kyrios*, equivalent to the Hebrew Adonay, which is a substitute for the unspoken JHVH.

For Christians the positive consequence of obedience to the Third Commandment is indicated in the prayer which, following the example of their Master, all Christians use. *Hallowed be thy name.* Were this petition to be truly understood, to be uttered in faith, with a lively expectation of God's

---

[1] Isaiah 55. 7.   [2] Isaiah 57, 15.   [3] Matt. 1. 21.
[4] Phil. 2. 9–11.

response, the consequences would be deep and far-reaching. For by the name of God we are to understand the character of God. As Dr. Charles put it, 'The name of God according to Hebrew usage stands for all that is known of God, and sums up all that God has made known of His nature, character and will.'[1] To pray *Hallowed be thy name* is therefore to be committed to His character, and to be committed to making that character known. Evangelism becomes inescapable. This is the positive Christian response to the negative command, *Thou shalt not take the name of the Lord thy God in vain, for the Lord will not hold him guiltless that taketh his name in vain.*

Not guiltless indeed; for the irreverent man has created a barrier between himself and God which will not disappear of its own volition, nor disappear as a result of man's striving. To remove the guilt of man action is needed. It is the Christian Good News that God has taken this action; that what man could not remove He has removed, but that His action is only effective for those who willingly accept both it and its consequences. 'Nothing in my hand I bring,' the Christian exclaims, knowing that the pierced hands of his Master have done what needed to be done; that He has done what He alone can do; and that the Lord will hold them guiltless that put their trust in Him.

It is not in words only that men take the name of God or of Christ in vain. It is also done through action. Christians were baptised in the name of the Father and the Son and the Holy Spirit, one God. They are members of a human association which proclaims itself the Body of Christ upon earth. When that society, by its manifest failure to be worthy of its name, draws upon itself the scorn of the world, when, for example, the words of Tertullian, *See how these Christians love one another*, are spoken with sarcastic intent, they are causing Christ's name to be taken in vain. For men are to

[1] *Op. cit.*, p. 90.

begin to learn the character of Christ from the lives and deeds of those who are His followers.

There will be much to be said about truth in a discussion of the Ninth Commandment, *Thou shalt not bear false witness against thy neighbour*. Here it is sufficient to point the connection between the two. If there be not truth in man's relationship to ultimate reality, there is not likely to be truth in his relations with his fellows. Sincerity in the one begets sincerity in the other.

IV

THE SABBATH AND THE STRANGER

Remember the Sabbath day to keep it holy. Six days shalt thou labour, and do all thy work: but the seventh day is a sabbath unto the Lord thy God: in it thou shalt not do any work, thou, nor thy son, nor thy daughter, thy manservant nor thy maidservant, nor thy cattle, nor thy stranger which is within thy gates: for in six days the Lord made heaven and earth, the sea and all that in them is, and rested the seventh day: wherefore the Lord blessed the seventh day and hallowed it. *Exodus 20. 8–11.*

But the seventh day is a sabbath unto the Lord thy God . . . that thy manservant and thy maidservant may rest as well as thou. And thou shalt remember that thou wast a servant in the land of Egypt, and the Lord thy God brought thee out thence by a mighty hand and by a stretched out arm: therefore the Lord thy God commanded thee to keep the sabbath day.

Deuteronomy 5. 14, 15.

And he said unto them, What man shall there be of you, that shall have one sheep, and if this fall into a pit on the sabbath day, will he not lay hold on it, and lift it out? How much then is a man of more value than a sheep! Wherefore it is lawful to do good on the sabbath day. *Matthew 12. 11, 12.*

The sabbath was made for man, and not man for the sabbath.

Mark 2. 27.

And for this cause did the Jews persecute Jesus, because he did these things on the sabbath day. But Jesus answered them, My Father worketh even until now, and I work. *John 5. 17.*

Now the first day of the week cometh Mary Magdalene early,

while it was yet dark, unto the tomb, and seeth the stone taken away from the tomb. *John 20. 1.*

And upon the first day of the week, when we were gathered together, to break bread. *Acts 20. 7.*

I was in the Spirit on the Lord's day. *Revelation 1. 10.*

By thine Agony and bloody Sweat; by thy Cross and Passion; by thy precious Death and Burial; by thy glorious Resurrection and Ascension; and by the coming of the Holy Ghost, *Good Lord, deliver us.*   *The Litany.*

———————

THE people of Israel meet us in many different guises in the biblical record. They are slaves in Egypt. They are nomads in the desert. The exact date of their settlement in the Nile delta and of the Exodus eludes historians and archaeologists; but its historicity can hardly be denied, for no people would invent so degrading a national origin. Nor can the period of their wanderings in the desert be dated; but it left as deep a mark upon their national character as the Exodus itself. They could never forget God's deliverance at the Red Sea. At the back of their consciousness they remained strangers and sojourners upon earth. Yet from the desert they turned to the settled lands of Canaan. Instead of being herdsmen, moving with their animals from oasis to oasis, they became agriculturalists, tending the vine, the fig tree and the olive, developing in time a city civilisation and a link through trade routes with the world's great empires. Resistance to these empires proved too much for them; and first the northern tribes were taken captive by Assyria, next the southern tribes by Babylon. Here some remembered Zion; with the homesickness of the exiled highlander; but many seemed to have forgotten. Yet it was among the minority, the minority that returned repentant to the Judæan hills, that the developments took place which created the Judaism of our Lord's day, the faith and practice of which so astonished the outside world, and still astonishes it.

There could be no Judaism without the Sabbath. The Sabbath the Jews believed, dated from their old nomadic days: it had been given at Sinai, in the wild places of Arabia. But it is clear that it could only begin to be fully kept when they had become a settled, agricultural people. Even then Sabbath keeping was neither complete nor always pleasing to the Almighty, the prophets declared. 'Bring no more vain oblations; incense is an abomination unto me; new moon and sabbath, the calling of assemblies, – I cannot away with inequity and the solemn meeting. Your new moons and your appointed feasts my soul hateth: they are a trouble to me; I am weary to bear them.'[1] It was only later, in exile in Babylon, when a design for a new order was being drawn up by men who looked back in penitence and looked forward in expectation, that a determination to enforce the Sabbath strictly was made: and it is from this time that the actual formulation of the Fourth Commandment as we have it to-day almost certainly derives. In the post-Exilic period, with the rise of Judaism, the Sabbath became what we find it in the Gospels, a national institution, enforced by minute regulations, accepted by public opinion, and made bearable by a series of legal fictions.

The Sabbath, added to the rejection of image-worship, enforced the position of the Jew as the enigma of the ancient world. Why this regular downing of tools on one day in seven, this refusal to walk more than a certain distance, to do anything that might be called work? This was sometimes carried to fantastic proportions. In the First Book of Maccabees there is recounted the successful uprising of the Jews against their

[1] Isaiah 1.13,14.

Syrian overlords rather more than a century and a half before the birth of Jesus. Early in the campaign, we read, their enemies 'set the battle in array against them on the sabbath day. And they said unto them, Thus far. Come forth and do according to the word of the king, and ye shall live. And they said, We will not come forth, neither will we do the word o the king to profane the sabbath day. And they hasted to give them battle. And they answered them not, neither cast a stone at them, nor stopped up the secret places, saying, Let us die all in our innocency: heaven and earth witness over us, that ye put us to death without trial. And they rose up against them in battle on the sabbath and they died, they and their wives and their children, and their cattle, to the number of a thousand souls.'[1] Later those in charge decided that this was no way to carry on a successful campaign; and that if they were attacked on the Sabbath they would reply. But how strong was the force of this inherited prohibition, this taboo, if you like, which allowed so many to be slain unresisting rather than protect themselves by breaking it. The story of these heroes was still being told in the days of Jesus. It lent authority to the pharisaic safeguarding of the holy day. It emphasised the shock men felt when Jesus announced, 'The sabbath was made for man, and not man for the sabbath; so that the Son of man is lord even of the sabbath.'[2]

The enigma of the ancient world – and of the modern world as well. Mr. Victor Gollancz has described in his autobiography what Sabbath observance meant to a boy brought up in an orthodox Jewish home in London in the early days of this century. On Friday evenings he had to walk from school in Hammersmith across London to Maida Vale because the Sabbath had already begun and he must not use a train. Nor must there be any contact – except through Gentile servants – with anything which might be classed, even derivatively, as fire. 'To stoke up the fire, or strike a

[1] 1. Macc. 2. 32–38.   [2] Mark 2. 27, 28.

match, or, worst of all, to smoke, would have been to "touch fire" derivatively.' There was a time, at the age of eight or nine, when his hobby was painting. Of course he could not do this on the Sabbath. (He had not even the outline texts to fill in, with which children in Evangelical homes were then familiar, published in a series entitled *Something for Sunday*.) But the day, which began at sundown on a Friday, ended at sundown on a Saturday. And he describes a scene from childhood which remains in his memory. 'On the mantel-piece, above a roaring fire, were my colours and a brush and a cupful of water; and I was standing with a watch in my hand, waiting for the exact second at which, on the authority of the "Jewish Chronicle" Sabbath would that day "go out" and at last I could paint. The exact second was every-thing; the previous second you *couldn't*, the following second you *could*.'[1]

The modern world finds this fantastic; so did the ancient world. It was fantastic, and yet, in a strange way, attractive. These people knew where they were. In the Roman Empire the synagogue worship attracted a certain number of Gen-tiles, who were impressed, no doubt, by the lofty mono-theism, the noble Scriptures of this people, how were attracted also, no doubt, by the Sabbath day, a haven of un-hurried quiet in the rush of life. And what of the present? Sometimes, on a summer's Sunday evening, as I wait minutes on the further side of the main road on which my vicarage is situated, endeavouring to anticipate some gap in the stream of motor traffic returning from the sea-coast, there occur to me lines about Sunday which had a place in the hymnal used in my childhood:

> 'Thou art a port protected
> From storms that round thee rise.'

To-day the English Sunday is a port invaded by landing-

[1] *My Dear Timothy* (London, 1952), pp. 45–48.

craft and heavily-armed troops; a day, for many people, not of quiet but of noise, not of rest but of restlessness. In Western Germany in 1956, the Federal Ministry of Transport announced that from May 1st lorries would no longer be allowed to travel on the German roads on Sundays because there was 'a national demand for peace and quiet on Sundays and holidays.'[1] It might appear that the 'Continental Sunday', which nineteenth-century Britain reprobated, and which twentieth-century Britain is fast adopting, is not quite so popular in the lands of its origin. 'Fifty-two "bank holidays" in the year would be destructive of all the best possibilities of Sunday, and almost infinitely mischievous,' wrote Bishop Hensley Henson.[2] We have to deal with a situation in which that mischief is far more securely established than when he wrote. If it be true, as has been said, that 'almost the greatest question of the time is the one of finding wells for the refreshment of our vitality',[3] have we not something to learn from this people which found, and finds, such a well once a week? Do we not need to down tools, or, to use modern elaborate language, to effect a moratorium on all unnecessary activity? The rhythm of labour and rest represents a natural need of man, which Christians still endeavour to safeguard for others as well as for themselves. This lies behind all the confused legislation and the annoying restrictions, which still prevent the English Sunday from becoming just a weekly bank holiday.

In the Law of Moses, or Pentateuch, as it is often called, there are two different interpretations of the Sabbath, which are partly in conflict with each other. The one with which we are most familiar comes in the version of the Fourth Commandment in Exodus 20, verses 8 to 11.

'Remember the sabbath day, to keep it holy.

[1] *Manchester Guardian*, April 7, 1956.
[2] *Bishoprick Papaers* (London, 1946), p. 275.
[3] W. R. Lethaby, *Form in Civilisation* (London, 1922), p.2.

Six days shalt thou labour, and do all thy work. But the seventh day is a sabbath unto the Lord thy God: in it thou shalt not do any work, thou, nor thy son nor thy daughter, thy manservant nor thy maidservant, nor thy cattle, nor thy stranger that is within thy gates: *for in six days the Lord made heaven and earth, the sea, and all that in them is, and rested the seventh day: wherefore the Lord blessed the sabbath day and hallowed it.*

The other interpretation is to be found in a different version of the Commandments, in the Book of Deuteronomy, chapter 5, verses 12 to 15.

'Observe the sabbath day to keep it holy, as the Lord thy God commanded thee.

Six days shalt thou labour, and do all thy work: but the seventh day is a sabbath unto the Lord thy God: in it thou shalt not do any work, thou, nor thy son, nor thy daughter, nor thine ox, nor thine ass, nor any of thy cattle, nor thy stranger that is within thy gates; *that thy manservant and thy maidservant may rest as well as thee. And thou shalt remember that thou wast a servant in the land of Egypt, and the Lord thy God brought thee out thence by a mighty hand and by a stretched out arm: therefore the Lord thy God commanded thee to keep the sabbath day.'*

The italicised words make it clear that Exodus sees the origin of the Sabbath in a commemoration of God's rest; that Deuteronomy sees it in the needs of men, in consideration of the lowly, in a recollection that those who were bidden keep this commandment had themselves been raised from an exceedingly lowly station. The version in Deuteronomy is actually older than the one in Exodus, as we now have it. Moreover, it was through developing the ideas latent in the conception of God resting after creation that there arose the exaggerated reverence for the Sabbath present in pharisaic Judaism. 'Regarded from this standpoint the Sabbath was an observance, obviously not made for man, but one that had its origin in the needs of the Godhead. If the Sabbath was observed originally to meet a necessity of God himself, then all beings created in His image would naturally be subject in some measure to the same necessity, and therefore all men would be under an everlasting obligation to keep the Sabbath. But since this revelation was originally made to Israel alone, Israel alone amongst mankind was originally subject to this obligation. This revelation to Israel therefore constituted a peculiar bond and everlasting sign between God and Israel.[1] So conceived, the Sabbath was in no case made for man, whereas in a very essential sense it would hold true that man was made for the Sabbath.'[2]

The teaching of Jesus appears therefore to be an appeal from a later tradition to an earlier one, which found the origin of the Sabbath not in the needs of God but in those of man. This lends to His saying discussed above, as it does to His defence of what critics regarded as Sabbath breaking: 'My Father worketh even until now, and I work.'[3] God had not created the universe and then stopped doing anything. He was always at work maintaining it. The Christ was now reflecting on earth the activity of the Father, and not pausing to ask whether a good act were done on the Sabbath day or not. (And it is for the Body of Christ to continue on earth the work of Christ.) It is interesting also that an early manuscript, *Codex Bezae (D)* preserves this addition to St. Luke 6. 4. 'On the same day, seeing a man working on the sabbath, he said unto him, If, O man, thou knowest what thou art doing, blessed art thou. But if thou dost not know, thou art accursed, and a transgressor of the law.' We understand also how Jesus looked with anger upon those opponents who watched Him to see whether He would heal a man on

[1] Exod. 31. 13, 17, Ezek. 20. 12, 20.
[2] R. H. Charles, *op. cit.*, p. 121.
[3] John 5. 17.

the Sabbath day.[1] Self-interest could always find a way out
of the Sabbath obligation if it were absolutely necessary.
'What man shall there be of you, that shall have one sheep,
and if this fall into a pit on the sabbath day, will he not lay
hold on it, and lift it out? How much then is a man of more
value than a sheep! Wherefore it is lawful to do good on the
sabbath day.'[2] The Sabbath, according to Deuteronomy,
arose in part from considerations of humanity to strangers
and servants. It was hypocrisy to make it a burden upon
others, but to be ready to break it when one's own property
was in danger.

Implicit, indeed, in both accounts of the institution of the
Sabbath is an active concern for the stranger, the fatherless,
the widow, for the man who is down on his luck, who thinks
he has no friends. Nor are these people to be approached in
any patronising spirit; but always with a recollection of the
ups and downs of life; with a remembrance that those who
were now up had once been down. The Israelite was to be
humble as he remembered his past and realised that the
favour in which he stood before God was due to God's grace
alone. 'Thou shalt remember that thou wast a servant in the
land of Egypt, and the Lord thy God brought thee out
thence by a mighty hand. . . . The Lord did not set his love
upon you, nor choose you, because you were more in number
than any people; for ye were the fewest of all peoples: but
because the Lord loveth you, and because he would keep the
oath which he sware unto your fathers.'[3] For a people so
circumstanced pride was the worst of sins; for pride is
always a rejection of God's grace, a breaking, therefore, of
the relationship between man and God. The best safeguards
against pride were first to remember their lowly origins and
secondly to confront themselves with the needs of others.

There is much about strangers in the Jewish Law, not
least in the remarkable nineteenth chapter of Leviticus,

[1] Mark 3, 2, 5.   [2] Matt. 12. 11, 12.   [3] Deut. 5. 15, & 7. 7, 8.

from which Jesus took the precept, 'Thou shalt love thy neighbour as thyself.'[1] It is often pointed out that this cannot have meant more originally than one's fellow-Israelite; and this may well be so. But one has only to read further in the chapter to discover that a wider compassion is intended. 'And if a stranger sojourn with thee in your land, ye shall not do him wrong. The stranger that sojourneth with you shall be as the homeborn among you, and thou shalt love him as thyself; for ye were strangers in the land of Egypt: I am the Lord your God.'[2] Again the Israelite is brought face to face with history and with the Almighty; and is called, in the light of both, to be a man of mercy and of charity. This was the principle of Sabbath-keeping, forgotten or over-laid, which Jesus re-emphasised to the discomfiture of His opponents.

It is the insistent temptation of a people that is conscious of its being called by God to imagine that this was occasioned by some special merit of its own, and to forget that privilege implies responsibility. Against this there stands the classic protest of Amos: 'You only have I known of all the families of the earth: therefore I will visit upon you all your iniquities . . . Are ye not as the children of the Ethiopians unto me, O children of Israel? saith the Lord. Have I not brought up Israel out of the land of Egypt, and the Philistines from Caphtor, and the Syrians from Kir?'[3] John the Baptist showed that he belonged to the same prophetic succession when he declared: 'begin not to say within yourselves, We have Abraham to our father: for I say unto you that God is able of these stones to raise up children unto Abraham.'[4] When the late Rudyard Kipling, in his most famous and moving poem, used the phrase, 'lesser breeds without the Law' he was employing an Old Testament conception which the most forward-looking prophets of the Old Testament

---

[1] Lev. 19. 18.   [2] Lev. 19. 33, 34.
[3] Amos 3. 2. and 9. 7.   [4] Luke 3. 8.

had themselves discarded as unworthy. Yet, despite the noble protests of the Second Isaiah and the author of Jonah, and of many later Rabbis, the Jews who made post-exilic Judiasm were so much on the defensive that they developed the close-fisted nationalism which we encounter in the Gospels.

It is one of the peculiar glories of the early Church that it created a new society in which all the fundamental antagonisms were overcome. 'There can be neither Jew nor Greek, there can be neither bond nor free, there can be no male and female: for ye are all one man in Christ Jesus.'[1] But the temptation which attacked Judaism has attacked Christianity, so that Christian witness in face of racial discrimination, though sometimes courageous, is more often equivocal, and sometimes appears to be a direct repudiation of the Christian tradition. The *predikants* of the Dutch Reformed Church in South Africa, are, we are told, 'often men of outstanding intellect and probity who are idealists – and apostles of *apartheid*.'[2] They can see no solution for the problems of South Africa – where black outnumbers white by thirteen to two – except in a rigid separation of the two. This is supported by a theology which seems to place the authority of the myth of the Tower of Babel above that of the Gospels:

'To create a cosmos God separated things; light from darkness, waters above the firmament from waters under the firmament, dry land from the sea. All living creatures too, he created *according to their kind* . . . From the very beginning it was the intention of the Lord that mankind should live in separate nations and peoples. In his sinful self-conceit man wished to frustrate this intention, as much as to say: "Let us not part, let us remain together. And let us build a tower to reach unto heaven.' And then God came as the Maker of separations and said: "Behold, the people is one, and they have all one language. Go to,

[1] Gal. 3. 28. Cf. Col. 3. 11.
[2] Colin Welch in *Encounter*, February, 1957.

let us go down and there confound their language! . . . So the Lord scattered them abroad. . . .

The rise and continuance of separate people and nations is, according to Scripture, in accordance with the will of God. Attempts at unification, the equalitarian idea, is a revival of the Babylonish spirit . . . Even in the Church of Christ, as it exists here in its instituted form, the Gospel did not abolish the difference in endowment, nature, culture, etc., between the different racial groups. Any attempt to ignore this will be an attempt to build another Tower of Babel.'[1]

The ingenuity of this theological justification for *apartheid* on earth – though not in Heaven – would be engaging were its consequences less serious. Examination shows that it is no more true to the Old Testament than to the New. At any rate, 'the Old Testament knows nothing of races which are "naturally inferior" or unworthy of designation as human, just as the dividing wall between Greeks and barbarians, or between master races and slave natures, which was never overcome in the ancient world, is completely foreign to it.'[1] It is true that some cosmopolitanism may be irreligious, Babylonish, even. But Jesus was crucified to draw men of all nations to Himself. In the New Israel there are no racial barriers. In Christian co-operation peoples of different national endowments can discover afresh the value of those endowments and the contribution they can make to the common service of God and men.

The great problem of our day has been stated in these terms: 'How will the economically and politically dominant 700 million people who call themselves "white" respond to the pressing demands for advance from the 1,700 millions

[1] Ds. C. B. Brink, the Moderator of the Church of the Transvaal, quoted Norman Goodall, *The Challenge of the Pretoria Conference*, in the *Ecumenical Review* (Geneva), July, 1954.

[1] Walter Eichrodt, *Man in the Old Testament* (London, 1951), p. 36. Cf. also G. W. Broomfield, *The Chosen People* (London), 1954.

who are called "coloured"?[1] It is a problem of which
many people are becoming rapidly aware in Britain as they
see non-European faces in their streets. The situation is
fairly easy when the stranger within the gates is a compara-
tive rarity, a curiosity to be accepted, made much of. Difficulties increase as numbers increase; when, in the United
States, Jews or Negroes, or Puerto Ricans filter into a district
and begin to take it over; or when the immigrant ships bring
growing numbers of dark-skinned Jamaicans, or West
Africans proud that they are members of the Commonwealth,
to London and the industrial centres of Britain. 'The stranger
that sojourneth with you shall be as the home born among
you, and thou shalt love him as thyself'[2] – not so easy when
men and women fear for their jobs and their standard of
living; not so easy, and all the more necessary. There was an
occasion, ludicrous had it not been tragic, when miners
from a pit which had recently refused to accept Italian labour,
marched on May Day behind an enormous banner inscribed
Workers of the World Unite! It never does for any people to
congratulate themselves upon freedom from racial discrimination, upon the absence of a colour bar. They may not
know the compulsive fears which motivate others, because
the occasion of those fears is not present: when they do feel
a threat to their own security they may behave in a similar
way. The way of life which the Commandments outline
makes very great demands; greater demands than unaided
human nature can bear. The achievement of a multi-racial
society is one of the pressing needs of our time. It needs,
above all else, the grace of God.

Nor is an imaginative concern for others to be limited to
people in the immediate neighbourhood. The world itself is
potentially a neighbourhood. Those who live in what are
primarily industrial countries draw their raw materials from

[1] Anthony H. Richmond, *The Colour Problem* (London, 1955), p. 11.

[2] Lev. 19. 33.

other lands, and export to them their finished products. No thinking Christian in England can be unconcerned about the situation in the West Indies, which has set so many of their inhabitants on the move. The twentieth century has also been called the Century of the Refugee. There is needed a care not only for the stranger within the gates but for those who would like to be strangers within our gates; but are debarred from entering by immigration quotas, labour permits and all the unneighbourly regulations that modern administration has devised. In some countries there has been a ready welcome for the young and the able-bodied; but a rejection of the disabled and the old – of all whom might in time become a charge upon the country of their adoption. The appalling phrase *hard core refugees* has become current to describe the human leavings after the labour market has been picked over by interested countries. Never was there greater need for mercy in human relationships than to-day. And there are no places where mercy more needs to be localised than in the refugee camps of Europe.

We may seem to have travelled far from the Sabbath; but we have been following a principle which the original founding of the Sabbath implied. In these days, it hardly needs to be said, when Christians speak of the Sabbath Day they are more often thinking of the first day of the week than of the seventh: they are thinking of Sunday, which has links with the Sabbath, but is a quite different festival. The Hebrew Sabbath was rooted in remembrance. ' *Thou shalt remember* that thou wast a servant in the land of Egypt, and the Lord thy God brought thee out thence by a mighty hand and a stretched out arm; therefore the Lord thy God commanded thee to keep the Sabbath Day.' Christians, on their festival day, recall a greater deliverance still, when God 'delivered us out of the power of darkness and translated us into the kingdom of the Son of his love.'[1] That deliverance was wrought

[1] Col. 1. 13.

by Christ's rising from the dead on the first day of the week. This was *the Lord's day* from the first. 'Jewish Christians would at first observe both the Sabbath on Saturday, and "the first day of the week" on the day of the Lord's Resurrection. Gentile Christians never, as far as we know, observed the Sabbath at all.' So wrote the late Dr. H. L. Goudge,[1] commenting on the instruction in 1 Corinthians 16. 2.: 'Upon the first day of the week let each one of you lay by him in store' for the collection for needy brethren in Jerusalem. It is significant that this follows upon St. Paul's great passage on the resurrection of Christ. And in the Book of Revelation we read, 'I was in the Spirit on the Lord's Day.'[2]

It is evidence of how much the resurrection meant to the first Christians that it caused them to change the day on which they went to church; the kind of thing about which worshippers are fiercely conservative, as anyone responsible for public worship has discovered when he has been hardy enough to change the hour of service. Sunday is not primarily a continuance of the Jewish Sabbath: it is a joyful new beginning; a day of rejoicing for the day that changed all history and the presence that can fill the humblest existence with meaning. Yet the two traditions intermingle in Christian history. We find them both in a prayer issued in the proposed Prayer Book of 1928, *For the observance of Sunday :*

Almighty God who hast given a day of rest to thy people, and, through thy Spirit in the Church, hast consecrated the first day of the week to be a perpetual memorial of thy Son's resurrection: Grant that we may so use thy gift that refreshed and strengthened in soul and body, we may serve thee faithfully all the days of our life.

All the days of our life. We cannot give all our days to worship: we give one, so that worship may be forgotten on none of them. The consecration of one consecrates all. This is a

---

[1] *Op. cit.*, p. 167.   [2] Rev. 1. 10.

principle reiterated in modern Anglican teaching, expressed often by Archbishop Temple. The Puritans, on the other hand, tended to believe that time itself was evil; that the Lord's Day, captured out of the sinful flux of time, alone was good. In consequence their rigorist excesses sometimes came near equalling those of the Jews, prompting the ridicule of a Puritan

> *Hanging of his cat on Monday*
> *For killing of a mouse on Sunday.*

On the other hand, in the same period, in 1618, James I issued his *Book of Sports*, saying that 'as for our good people's lawful recreation, our good pleasure likewise is, that after the end of divine service our good people be not disturbed, letted or discouraged from any lawful recreation, such as dancing, either men or women; archery for men, leaping, vaulting, or any other such harmless recreation.' He goes on to catalogue these; and adds that those in authority must 'punish all such, as in abuse of this our liberty, will use these exercises before the end of all divine services for that day: and we likewise straightly command that every person shall resort to his own parish church to hear divine service, and each parish by itself to use the said recreation after divine service.'[1] The King ordered that this – and much more – should be read aloud from the pulpit of every church. So many clergy refused that the book was withdrawn; to be re-issued by Charles I in 1633.

These conflicting attitudes to Sunday have continued in English history; though the puritanical one was long uppermost, to the considerable astonishment, not to say discomfiture of visitors from the Continent. Even the Prince Consort, upon his arrival in England, told Archdeacon Wilberforce that he thought the English Sunday was dull, complaining of the lack of innocent amusements in England

[1] *Documents of the Christian Church*, selected and edited by Henry Bettenson (London, 1943), p. 387 ff.

for the common people. Later the Archdeacon – now Bishop of Oxford – was himself criticised because he had been present when the Prince played chess on a Sunday, and had not raised his voice in protest.[1] We have altered all that. But reactions need to be watched, lest they go too far: and it would be well to estimate what are the right principles for a Christian use of Sunday, and how far those principles should affect people whose membership of the Church is nominal or non-existent.

The following seem clear:

First, Sunday should be a day of worship; a day when the opportunity of worship and the invitation to worship is offered to all; a day when the family of the Church comes together as a family to thank God for His goodness, to hear more of His truth, to be empowered and directed for His service. No mere private worship can take the place of this. Indeed the local congregation needs constantly to be reminded that it is part of the universal family of Christ which, on that day, in country after country as the sunlight passes round the world, is giving praise to God.

Secondly, Sunday should at least be a day of rest in the sense that Christians do not cause others to do unnecessary work for them. Here is a criterion to be applied to Sunday amusements. There are other modern practices which need to be examined, not merely by those who employ others, or profit from their labours, but by the workers themselves. It is said that the commonest question asked nowadays when people take on a new job is 'What overtime work is there?' The inquiry is not about something to be avoided but rather welcomed for its increased rates of pay. Much of this overtime work falls on Sundays.

Thirdly, Sunday should be a day of real recreation; which by its changed occupations refreshes the mind and body and

[1] G. W. Daniell, *Bishop Wilberforce* (Leaders of Religion, London 1891), pp. 32 & 89.

spirit. James I was right in principle when he permitted recreation *after divine service*. Important too was his insistence that these recreations should be in the people's own parish; thus avoiding the restless and largely aimless travelling of to-day, and the assembling of large multitudes, He could not have forseen men queueing for the greater part of a Sunday to obtain cup-tie tickets.

The writers of the Shorter Catechism in 1643 excepted from the restrictions of Sunday 'works of necessity *and mercy*.' Doing works of mercy is to follow the example of Jesus Christ; to use Sunday as He used the Sabbath. Similarly Jeremy Taylor, writing in the time of the Commonwealth, concludes his catalogue of how Sunday is to be spent with 'reconciling enmities, remission of burdens and of offences, of debts and of work; friendly offices, neighbourhood, and provoking one another to good works.'[1]

This should be a day when a Christian goes out of his way to help those who are in need. And there is much to be said for making Sunday a family day, a day when the family is at home to others; though little is to be said for the common practice of putting family gatherings in the place of worship. What we need is to see the family united in the larger Family in their Father's house. Christian hospitality which went as far as this might bring many people back to the worship of the Church.

For Christians Sunday is the most important day of the week. A week without Sunday can be like a ship without a rudder. On the Lord's Day Christians come together into the presence of their Lord: it is here that the Christian family realises its unity as at few other times. This does not happen automatically. Sunday must be *remembered*. But if it be also hallowed it may hallow all the week.

[1] Holy Dying, ch. 4, sect. 7.

V

PARENTS AND CHILDREN

Honour thy father and thy mother: that thy days may be long in the land which the Lord thy God giveth thee. *Exodus 20. 12.*

Children, obey your parents in the Lord: for this is right. Honour thy father and thy mother (which is the first commandment with promise), that it may be well with thee, and that thou mayest live long on the earth. And ye fathers, provoke not your children to wrath: but nurture them in the chastening and admonition of the Lord. *Ephesians 6. 1–4.*

A father of the fatherless, and a judge of the widows is God in his holy habitation. God setteth the solitary in families.

Psalm 68. 5, 6.

Young men and maidens, old men and children, praise the Name of the Lord: for his Name only is excellent, and his praise above heaven and earth. *Psalm 148. 12.*

When my father and my mother forsake me: the Lord taketh me up. *Psalm 27. 12.*

And he went down with them, and came to Nazareth; and he was subject unto them: and his mother kept all these saying in her heart. And Jesus advanced in wisdom and stature, and in favour with God and man. *Luke 2. 51–52.*

Jesus said, Verily I say unto you, There is no man that hath left house, or brethren, or sisters, or mother, or father, or children, or lands, for my sake, and for the gospels' sake, but he shall receive a hundredfold now in this time, houses, and brethren, and sisters, and mothers, and children, and lands, with persecutions; and in the world to come eternal life. *Mark 10. 29, 30.*

When Jesus therefore saw his mother, and the disciple standing by whom he loved, he saith unto his mother, Woman, behold thy son! Then saith he to the disciple, Behold thy mother! And from that hour the disciple took her into his own home.

John 19. 26, 27.

Bless, O Lord, the families of our nation, that children and parents, honouring each other, may honour thee, and, by the service of our lives, the land which thou hast given us be made thine: through Jesus Christ our Lord. Amen.

———————

THE command to keep the weekly Sabbath had notable implications for strangers and foreigners. It presumed a fellowship of all men as God's creatures, which, as Bishop Gore put it, was 'developed in the New Testament into the principle that each man has a right to equal consideration, that each man counts for one, and nobody for more than one.'[1] The Hebrews themselves were never to forget, not only that they had been strangers in the land of Egypt, but that strangers they remained, even in the land of promise. Their delivery from oppression and their identity as a nation was due, not to some democratic upsurge of enthusiasm, but to the mighty acts of God. In time they became a settled people; but they could never forget that they had been nomads. (Even at a modern Passover, when the father of the family breaks the unleavened bread, he says, 'This is the bread of affliction which your fathers did eat in the land of Egypt.') They might build houses of clay and stone; but they would always remember that they had been dwellers in tents.

Recollection of these early, humble, migratory days induced a sense of humility and of the transitoriness of life.

[1] *The Sermon on the Mount,* p. 211.

Strangers and sojourners, the recurring phrase represents a dominant Old Testament theme.[1] A Christian writer also, looking back over the heroes of the earlier times, who had prepared the way for the fuller revelation in the Messiah, could declare, 'These all died in faith, not having received the promises, but having seen them and greeted them from afar, and having confessed that they were strangers and pilgrims on the earth.'[2] The Christian's sense that he has here no continuing city is derived ultimately from people who lived in real tents, the pivot of whose lives were oases in the desert.

Migratory people develop certain characteristics. As Dr. T. H. Robinson has pointed out it was important for Israel that 'her ideal ancestors belonged to an order of society in which the value of persons far outweighed that of things. There was a passion for freedom, a love of independence, an impatience of external control, which distinguish the shepherd races from those of more settled lands. . . . To one another the members of the tribe were brethren, and while they might accept the command of one of their number for special occasions, such as war, the restraints of authority were unnatural to them.'[3] Even in modern times few can return from a camping holiday without having learned some lessons in corporate inter-dependence. People on the move, like the Israelites – or like settlers moving across the plains of America in covered wagons – find their pace set by the weakest and the oldest. The able-bodied may go forward as scouts; but they must constantly return to a slowly-moving base. They may be tempted to jettison the aged and the sick; but they can hardly do this because of the force of public opinion. In nomadic life, for all its impatience of external control, a man is not so much an individual as a member of a

[1] Lev. 25. 23, 1. Chron. 29. 15, Psalm 39. 12.
[2] Heb. 11. 13.
[3] *Op. cit.*, vol. 1, p. 105.

family: he would not question the modern theological assertion that the family is the basic unit of society. The state is a comparatively modern development, but the family has always been there. Scholars may find difficulty in fitting the law of Sabbath observance into the days of desert wandering; but to that setting the Fifth Commandment unquestionably belongs. *Honour thy father and thy mother, that thy days may be long in the land which the Lord thy God giveth thee.* The promise of the conclusion may be a later addition: but the command to honour parents has not only a desert background; it represents a desert necessity.

In a nomadic society everyone has his place, else society falls to pieces. In many parts of the world to-day society has acquired a mobility which is comparable to nomadism, but which is without the traditional restraints of nomad life. In so stable a country as Britain the varying demands of industry, creating labour shortages in one place, and redundancy in another, have made many people strangers and sojourners, in housing estates, lodgings and caravans. When a family moves to a centre of better employment, are the old people to go too, to sever accustomed ties for they know not what? The wide-spreading new estates, whether provided by local authorities or by private enterprise, do not always increase stability; and they make most wage-earners travellers for a considerable proportion of their day. A people on the move may not find it difficult to honour father and mother: what is more difficult is to honour grandfather and grandmother; to provide a place for them in the human family and in the council house. There is a constant complaint that institutional provision for old people is far too limited. But old people do not want to go into institutions, however well run they may be. They want to stay at home. Their desire is to be integrated with society, not isolated from it. Their hunger is for respect, to be honoured.

An emphasis on care for the weak and aged runs through

the Jewish Law; and, as a complement, the hope of an honoured old age is dominant in the Psalms and Wisdom literature.

> Blessed is every one that feareth the Lord,
> That walketh in his ways.
> For thou shalt eat the labour of thine hands:
> Happy shalt thou be, and it shall be well with thee.
> Thy wife shall be as a fruitful vine, in the innermost
>   parts of thine house:
> Thy children like olive plants, round about thy table.
> Behold, that thus shall the man be blessed
> That feareth the Lord.[1]

This patriarchal ideal remained in our Lord's day, and it is still present in Judaism. But that there were ways of evading filial responsibility is indicated by a famous passage in St. Mark:

> 'And he said to them, "You have a fine way of rejecting the commandment of God, in order to keep your tradition! For Moses said, "Honour your father and your mother'; and 'He who speaks evil of father or mother, let him surely die'; but you say, 'If a man tell his father or his mother, What you would have gained from me is Corban' (that is, given to God) – then you no longer permit him to do anything for his father or mother, thus making void the word of God through your tradition which you hand on. And many such things you do."'[2]

Modern Jewish scholars have taken exception to this, and have pointed out that 'according to Rabbinic law as codified in the Mishnah, and commented on in the Talmud, the Rabbis are on the side of Jesus and take this very line.[3] It is

[1] Psalm 128. 1–4.

[2] Mark. 7. 9–11. (Revised Standard Version).

[3] C. G. Montefiore, quoted Vincent Taylor, *St. Mark* (London, 1952), p. 342.

unlikely, however, that the Christian community would have preserved this rather unusual saying if it had no foundation in fact. There may have been, as Dr. Rawlinson suggests, some *cause célèbre* to which Jesus was referring.[1] The infamy He condemned was that of using a secondary religious obligation to defeat a primary one. The warning remains, for every age has its own way of saying 'Corban'; of shuffling off inconvenient responsibilities with a show of virtuous action.

The temptation of patriarchal societies is the tyranny of the younger generation by the older one; a tryanny which tends to perpetuate itself, each generation deciding to 'take it out of' the younger one in revenge for the treatment to which it was formerly subjected. The rightful mutuality of relationship is expressed often by St. Paul, who emphasized both the responsibility of children to their parents and the responsibility of parents for and to their children. Sir William Ramsay once suggested that he had good personal reasons for insisting upon this double responsibility. In Philippians 3. 8. he speaks of 'Christ Jesus my lord for whom I suffered the loss of all things'; and it is at least a reasonable conjecture that when he returned to Tarsus as a Christian he was disinherited by his family, 'If Paul had to face such a scene, we can appreciate the reason why he lays so much stress on the duty of parents to respect their children's just feelings: "ye fathers, provoke not your children to wrath; but bring them up in the education and admonition of the Lord" (Eph. 6. 4.): "fathers, provoke not your children, lest they lose heart" (Col. 3. 21.) Not every person would think this one of the most important pieces of advice to give his young societies in Asia Minor. But, according to our conjecture, Paul had good cause to know the harm that parents may do by not reasonably considering their children's desires and beliefs. At the same time he strongly emphasizes in the same passage the duty of

[2] *St. Mark* (London, 1925), p. 95.

children to obey their parents, and sets this before the duty of parents to their children. That also is characteristic of one who had been blameless as touching all the commandments (Phil. 3. 6.), and who therefore must have gone to the fullest extreme in compliance with his father's orders before he announced that he could comply no further.'[1]

The modern world, no doubt, has many parallels to this conjectured event. Certainly the possessive parent – the possessive mother, most often – has wrecked many a modern marriage. An interesting study speaks of parents who *usurp* their children's lives, and quotes a children's officer as saying '"Parents are trustees for their children; yet so many think of themselves as owners." The most complete usurpers were these owner-parents; owner-drivers, too, of whom some drove the child openly, some, subtly; knowing what they were doing or unconsciously; in fear of them, or with what passed for love.' The dictionary meaning of usurpation is quoted as 'unjust encroachment on the rights of others.'[2] Too many parents, at a later stage, fail to accept the limitation expressed in the teaching of Jesus, 'for this cause shall a man leave his father and mother, and shall cleave to his wife.'[3] Those who fail in this way have probably more often been indulgent than repressive parents, though their indulgence has been in part self-indulgence. It is the indulgent parent who occasions most harm to-day; the parent whose children must always have the best, who denies them nothing, except the development of their own personalities in response to discipline. There are parents who feel in their bones that they ought not to be indulgent, who recall that they were brought up in quite another way, but who lack the courage to refuse. They may not themselves have any desire

[1] *St. Paul the Traveller and the Roman Citizen* (19th edit., London, 1942, p. 36.)

[2] Michael Burn, *Mr. Lyward's Answer* (London, 1956), p. 19.

[3] Matt. 19. 5.

to 'keep up with the Joneses' but they find it hard that their children should not be abreast of others. The pressure of public opinion is rarely so weighty as when it is expressed through the requests of children, as commercial advertisers realize very well. Moreover, to many parents, present-day children appear much abler and far more knowledgeable than they were at the same age – so why should not the children know better than their parents?

The rapid growth of education, and its provision out of public funds – instead of from family savings – has exacerbated the situation. The aims of educational reformers in Britain have not all been achieved; but the situation is very different from what it was even thirty years ago. After the War the Barlow Report recommended that the number of University students should be doubled; and this proposal has been found inadequate to meet the need. The University of Leeds, for example, had 1,700 students in 1939: in 1956 the number was 3,700: five years later it is expected to be 5,300 – with three thousand of them studying science or technology.[1] Inevitably this will cause cultural barriers between the generations. There will be many proud parents. It is important that there should be many sons and daughters who respect and honour parents who lacked the opportunities they have been granted. It is hardly less important that those whose studies are financed by the community should accept with gratitude what is given them and endeavour to see to it that as they have entered into other men's labours so others, in their turn, may enter into theirs.

In times of rapid social change youth represents a reservoir of uncommitted power which political and religious movements naturally wish to tap, so that their own future may be assured. In the countries of Africa and the East, where social change, for some at any rate, has been much more rapid than in the West, where changes and develop-

[1] *Manchester Guardian*, November 22, 1956.

ments which in Europe took centuries are being hustled through in decades, the student class has become more important than any other, the sharpened spearhead of revolutionary change. Students, and all young people, are wooed by Communism, Nationalism, Christianity, Islam. Instead of the exaggerated respect once paid to the aged an exaggerated respect may now be paid to the young. In totalitarian countries there have been two baleful manifestations of disobedience to the Fifth Commandment; the killing off of aged people whom the community can no longer afford to support, and the spying upon parents by their children on behalf of the secret police.

Other developments have affected the balance of family life. It has often been pointed out that in Britain until the eighteenth century the home was a producing unit: the family worked together in the family workshop. Something of this lingered on through the nineteenth to the twentieth century. Its last relic was, perhaps, the retail shop, with the family living over it, and assistants perhaps lodged on an attic floor. (Nowadays few people live over shops: in most towns only a small proportion of the retail businesses appear to be locally owned.) In time the home changed from being a producing to being a consuming unit; a place where meals were cooked and eaten, and family pleasures enjoyed. It looked for a period as if even this function were likely to be eclipsed, as more meals were eaten in canteens and restaurants, and more evenings spent in clubs and cinemas and public houses. The growing dominance of the shift system, which may mean that the son of the house works through the night, while his father works through the day, throws the family further out of balance. Nor is there much use of a family pew to provide a weekly integration. One of the good results of television is that it tethers people at home to watch a favourite programme instead of seeking diversion elsewhere.

All the Commandments, it has been pointed out, are based on loyalty. In the Decalogue 'the demand is made that Israel's loyalty to the Covenant should be shown not only in devotion of spirit to God, but in fundamental loyalty to one another. Loyalty to parents, and loyalty to one's neighbour – expressing itself in counting sacred his life, his wife, his property and his reputation – and the cultivation of a loyalty of spirit as well as of act, provide the terms wherein loyalty to God can be expressed.'[1] Of these loyalties that to the family can be earliest evoked, expressed and understood. In the human family a child can begin to learn the meaning of the divine family. For 'the God and Father of our Lord Jesus Christ' is the one 'of whom every family in heaven and on earth is named.'[2] St. Paul here makes a play upon words which is irrecoverable in an English translation; for in Greek the word *patria* meaning family, or tride, is directly derived from *pater* meaning father. A decay in family loyalties must inevitably make more difficult the proclamation of the Gospel: for it blunts the significance of that central analogy upon which true religion is based, that 'like as a father pitieth his own children, even so is the Lord merciful unto them that fear him.'[3]

A succession of reports on juvenile delinquency and kindred subjects has indicated that a part of the fault is to be found in adult delinquency, or, at least, in adult failure. The source is traced back again and again to the broken home, to the home where there is no love between parents and, sometimes, not even respect. Social workers, however, are usually quick to add that any form of home is better than none at all; that a background of continual bickering, even, can often provide a greater sense of security than the cool efficiency of an institution. There is much to suggest that the making of

[1] H. H. Rowley, *The Unity of the Bible* (London, 1935), p. 79.

[2] Eph. 3. 13, 14.

[3] Psalm 103. 13.

Christian homes is the battle of Britain to-day – a battle
which has to be won by couples. Earlier civilisations have
decayed because of a breakdown in family life; and that is a
present danger – so that a scanty supply of social workers,
marriage guidance counsellors, and, above all probation
officers, fulfil the function of white corpuscles in the blood
stream, struggling against and defeating disease. The promise *that thy days may be long in the land which the Lord thy
God giveth thee* has significance for the longevity and
creativity of civilisations. 'Honour thy father and thy
mother, as the Lord thy God commanded thee," is the version of the Fifth Commandment in Deuteronomy 5. 16
'that thy days may be long, *and that it may go well with thee*,
upon the land which the Lord thy God giveth thee.'

Reports on youth have been followed by reports on age;
and English people have been disturbed to discover that the
proportion of people past minimum pensionable age (65 for
men and 60 for women) is already much greater than ever
before, and will continue to grow. In 1911 the proportion of
these older people in the population was one in fifteen. In
1951 it had become two in fifteen. By 1977 it will be three in
fifteen. As the reader considers these figures and looks to the
future he realises that, unless his life be cut short, he will
himself be one of these older people in an ageing population.
What does he look forward to? There is much talk of
expectation of life nowadays; less talk about the kind of
life which people are to expect. There is much talk of the
welfare state; far less talk about what constitutes welfare.
These are some of the most important questions of our era;
they demand determined thought by older people who bring
to their perspective of life insights they have gained and are
gaining as disciples of Jesus Christ.

There is something very tragic about purposeless old age;
especially when people are not feeling old; when they are
kept out of the way, kept amused, but *not honoured*. The need

of a child and of an old age pensioner is fundamentally the same; it is a need for respect. Respect is more likely to be evoked when old people are performing a useful function, contributing to the community life, perhaps within the family, perhaps by continuing to go out to work. The suggestion that older people should remain in employment is easily made; not usually easily carried out. There are difficulties of adjustment where the pace of a factory is that of younger workers – and where much depends on pace. Not all jobs in a factory, either, are fitted to shorter hours of work by a special group of workers. If the older workers are allowed even to appear parasitic the intention which has led to their employment will be frustrated. Yet, despite the difficulties, more plans of this sort will have to be made, if every generation in the community is to be granted the honour which is its due.

We have said that a Christian uses the analogy of human fatherhood to understand the relationship of God to the world. We have to begin at the human side; but as we do so we have to remember that we are actually starting in the wrong place. Nothing in the life of God is derived from the life of man. The real fatherhood is God's fatherhood: the real family is His family. From the divine fatherhood all that is good in human parenthood is derived. And the command to honour father and mother is to honour those who, by the function they fulfil, dimly represent the relationship of God to His creatures. Through men and women made in His image we are led to the Maker Himself, from the human family to 'the God and Father of our Lord Jesus Christ, of whom every family in heaven and on earth is named.'

VI

THE SANCTITY OF LIFE

Thou shalt do no murder. *Exodus 20. 13.*

Whoso sheddeth man's blood, by man shall his blood be shed: for in the image of God made he man. *Genesis 9. 6.*

If thine enemy be hungry, give him bread to eat;
And if he be thirsty, give him water to drink:
For thou shalt heap coals of fire upon his head,
And the Lord shall reward thee. *Proverbs 25. 21, 22.*

Love worketh no ill to his neighbour: love therefore is the fulfilling of the law. *Romans 13. 10.*

Ye have heard that it was said to them of old time, Thou shalt not kill; and whosoever shall kill shall be in danger of the judgment: but I say unto you that every one who is angry with his brother shall be in danger of the judgment. *Matthew 5. 21, 22.*

Ye have heard that it was said, Thou shalt love thy neighbour, and hate thine enemy: but I say unto you, love your enemies, and pray for them that persecute you; that ye may be sons of your Father which is in heaven: for he maketh his sun to rise on the evil and the good, and sendeth rain on the just and the unjust
Matthew 5, 43–45.

For hereunto were ye called: because Christ also suffered for you, leaving you an example, that ye should follow his steps, who did no sin, neither was guile found in his mouth: who, when he was reviled, reviled not again; when he suffered, threatened not; but committed himself to him that judgeth righteously: who his they asked was whether their God had ordered them to do this or not; whether He were on their side – for if He were not, all their military preparations would appear foolishness, and all their military expeditions would be doomed to failure.

> *If it had not been the Lord who was on our side,*
> *Let Israel now say;*
> *If it had not been the Lord who was on our side,*
> *When men rose up against us :*
> *Then they had swallowed us up alive.*[1]

1. Kings 22 records the failure of an expedition when the Lord was not on the side of the allied kings of Israel and Judah, conspiring together to regain the outpost of Ramoth in Gilead by conquest. They were misled, not only by the ambition of Ahab, but by the 'lying spirit' in the mouth of the massed prophets, exultant in their nationalistic fervour, who exhorted them to go to the battle and prosper in the name of the Lord. On this occasion one prophet alone represented both sanity and the will of the Lord.

There is no pacifism in the Old Testament, nor any desire to abolish capital punishment. Indeed, as R. W. Dale pointed out, the first seven Commandments were themselves 'protected by the heaviest and sternest punishment which human law can inflict. The worship of any other God than Jehovah was punished with death. The worship of any image of Jehovah Himself was punished with death. Blasphemy was punished with death. Sabbath-breaking was punished with death. Determined resistance to the authority of parents, and the flagrant want of reverence for them, were punished with death. Adultery was punished with death.'[2] There are many provisions of this kind in the Books of the

---

[1] Psalm 124. 1–3.

[2] *The Ten Commandments* (Sixth Edition, London, 1891), p. 261.

Law, as well as the general statement, 'Whoso sheddeth man's blood, by man shall his blood be shed: for in the image of God made he man.'[1] This earliest reason for capital punishment is because murder is an insult to God. A man has been treated as though he were a thing, with which one can do what one likes, and not a person, unique and unrepeatable, bearing in his life not only an inheritance from his parents, and a capacity for fellowship with them, but an inheritenace from God and a capacity for fellowship with Him. Once bring God into the picture, and consider a responsibility to Him, and it becomes much more difficult to think of men and women in mechanical terms, as hands, or as forces to be wagered for a military objective. The conception of personality is already in the offing.

The New Testament is full of reverence for life as the gift of God. Those who passed by on the other side of the road from Jerusalem to Jericho, where lay a robbed and injured man, probably thought it more important to appear at worship in the Temple undefiled than to succour a fellow human being, made in the image of God. Such lack of proportion was condemned by Jesus. The Epistles go further and think of men as brothers for whom Christ died. Yet there is no policy of 'Safety First' in the Bible. When St. Paul was in prison – probably in Rome – his friends at Philippi sent one of their number to help him; a mission of aid which he prosecuted with such vigour that he was wearing himself out, and had made himself very ill. St. Paul sent this man Epaphroditus back to Philippi that his friends' anxiety might be relieved. He had been gambling with his life. The actual word used by St. Paul in Philippians 2. 30 may have occurred to him because he had often watched his Roman guards gambling for money. From it also came the name *parabolani* applied to brotherhoods in the early Church whose members hazarded their lives by caring for those who were victims of

[1] Genesis 9. 6.

the plague.[1] The prayer of St. Ignatius Loyola strikes an echo in most Christian experience: 'Teach us, Good Lord, to serve thee as thou deservest; to give and not to count the cost; to fight and not to heed the wounds; to toil and not to seek for rest; to labour and not to ask for any reward save that of knowing that we do thy will.' The way of discipleship is a way of the cross. Christians are followers of a Man who was murdered. They know that whosoever would save his life must lose it.

The Church was built on martyrdoms. 'It is not, therefore, man's physical life that is sacred, but the man himself. Physical life has only a relative degree of sacredness. There is a whole hierarchy of good things more sacred than physical life, and to preserve physical life at the cost of any one of these would be to make life itself a curse. For every man is infinitely more sacred than this passing phase of his existence.'[2] Yet the demands which a Christian may make upon himself are not demands which he can make upon his neighbour; unless they be commonly accepted within the deeply committed brotherhood of the Church. A Christian's life must always be outgoing, towards God and towards his neighbour. 'Care for the life of another, even material, bodily care, is spiritual in essence. Bread for myself is a material question: bread for my neighbour is a spiritual question.'[3] It were well for imaginations to be stretched to grasp what reverence for life should mean in the broken world of to-day. 'If we had but eyes to see,' says Dr. George Macleod, 'we all live in famine town to-day, in our unified world.'[4] When peoples are hungry, and when they are denied essential freedoms, they do desperate things. In many parts of

[1] These 'suicide squads' are described in Kingsley's *Hypatia*.

[2] R. H. Charles, *op. cit.*, p. 196.

[3] Nicholas Berdyaev, *The Fate of Man in the Modern World* (London, 1935), p. 120.

[4] *Only One Way Left* (Glasgow, 1956), p. 113.

Eastern Europe there is a desire for uprising – and Hungary has shown us what uprising can cost, and yet be ineffective. Among many exiled peoples there is a desire, and there are probably plans, for a war of revenge. In former days popular uprisings against tyranny had a fair chance of success. The situation is different to-day, when an issue is not likely to be decided by muskets or rifles, but by potent modern weapons which insurrectionists can usually neither obtain nor afford.

People shrink from war, not necessarily because they are convinced that it is wrong, but because it is so intolerably destructive. The old talk about unsheathing the sword and keeping the flag flying will fool some of the people some of the time: but not so many as formerly; for swords nowadays are only ornamental, and ordinary people are thinking more about deep shelters. In the thirty-seventh of the Thirty-Nine Articles in the *Book of Common Prayer* pacifism is specifically repudiated. 'It is lawful for Christian men, at the commandment of the Magistrate, to wear weapons and to serve in the wars.' That may have seemed unexceptionable in the sixteenth century; though the fact that it had to be said indicated that some people's consciences were troubled. Pacifist sects were on their way; prompted, no doubt, by a discovery that in the early says of the Church there were Christians who refused to take arms against their enemies; while the thought of Christians fighting against Christians was intolerable.

War, many Christians believe, is only defensible if it serves to prevent what is worse than war. That was what many felt in 1939. Nothing could be worse than that our children – or any children, for that matter – should be brought up to worship the false gods of Nazism. But warfare has an unpleasant way of making the defenders of righteousness approximate, in ways which would previously have appalled them, to what they are opposing. When the first Zeppelin raids took place over London in 1916, King George V visited wounded civilians in Charing Cross Hospital. 'It is simple murder,' he wrote in his diary afterwards.[1] Is there any 'total' war which is not 'simple murder'? The biographer of King George, who has preserved this comment, records also, in a footnote, a contrast between the use of ammunition in the South African War and in that of 1914–1918. 'In the whole of the South African War 273,000 rounds had been fired. One million rounds were expended in the first six months of the 1914–1918 war. By November 1916 the consumption rose to 1,120,000 a week.'[2] In more recent conflict those who were shocked by the bombing of Coventry proceeded to obliteration bombing of Hamburg. The ruins of London and Hull were terrifying – until one had seen more terrifying ones in Rotterdam and the Ruhr. Nor was it only that war had become more terrifying through the use of more potent weapons. It had also become ideological. Even in the midst of the Napoleonic Wars there was a certain amount of contact between Britain and France: in the wars of earlier centuries this contact was assumed by men of culture and letters, hardly interrupted though soldiers and sailors were fighting.

Nowadays, as always when warfare is being discussed, much use is made of comparison with the action of the police. But for the Christian conscience the question is whether a police action of this kind can ever be that and no more. After all the arms supplied to the police are limited. Where is the dividing line which separates warfare from murder? Those, moreover, who have seen films of the results of the atom bomb on Hiroshima cannot with an untroubled conscience approve the production of even more powerfully destructive weapons, whose use would threaten unborn generations and might involve a threat to life itself. There is needed a deep

[1] Harold Nicolson, *King George V* (London, 1952), p. 272.
[2] *Ibid.*, p. 261, n.

and deepening reverence for life as the unique and irreplace-
able gift of God.

These things trouble the conscience of Christian thinkers,
especially when they meet in international conferences,
pacifists and non-pacifists from different countries side by
side. Easy enough to agree that war as a means of settling
political disputes in incompatible with the will of God. Easy
also to proclaim that in Christian thought peace is no mere
absence of war, but something much more positive and
creative. Easy also to say that there is great need for further
examination of this vital issue by theologians.[1] Comparatively easy, even, to 'call upon the nations to pledge that
they will refrain from the threat or use of hydrogen, atomic,
and all other weapons of mass destruction as well as any
other means of force against the territorial integrity of any
state.'[2] But when the question is asked, 'What does "A" do
next? Does he refuse to serve in the Forces?' the answer is
still left to the individual conscience.

Yet there are some rays of hope. It is in face of world
conflict that the Church has realised itself afresh, and perhaps as never before, as a supra-national community. The
ecumenical Conference on Church, Community and State,
which met at Oxford in 1937, issued *A Message to the
Christian Churches*, which was largely the work of William
Temple, then Archbishop of York. In 1937 it did not seem
likely that war could be avoided: its prospect led the *Message*
to an emphasis which to many seemed novel. 'If war breaks
out, then pre-eminently the Church must manifestly be the
Church, still united as the one Body of Christ, though the
nations wherein it is planted fight one another, consciously
offering the same prayers that God's Name may be hallowed,
His Kingdom come, and His Will be done in both, or all,

[1] *The First Assembly of the World Council of Churches. Official Report*
(London, 1949), p. 90.
[2] *The Evanston Report*—The Second Assembly of the World Council
of Churches (London, 1955), p. 133.

the warring nations. The fellowship of prayer must at all costs remain unbroken. The Church must also hold together in one spiritual fellowship those of its members who take different views concerning their duty as Christian citizens in time of war.'[1] In the succeeding years this hope was not wholly betrayed. After the 1914–1918 war it was six years before the leaders of the French and German Protestant Churches really met, at the Stockholm Conference in 1925; and even then there was a deep rift between them because of the 'war guilt' clause in the Treaty of Versailles. After the Second World War it hardly took six months. Representatives met at Stuttgart in October, 1945. When a committee of the World Council of Churches, then only 'in process of formation', met at Geneva in March 1946, Bishop Berggrav of Norway made a confession: 'I wondered anxiously what it would be like to meet to-day with friends from all the different parts of the Christian world. The surprise, for me at any rate, was that it was no surprise. It was quite natural. Natural because we have lived together more closely during these five years than we did when we could communicate with the outside world. We have prayed together much more, we have listened more to God's Word, our hearts have been alongside one another.'

At the same meeting Dr. Martin Niemöller declared: 'During these past twelve years we have learned, we Christians in Germany – and with what gratitude – that we were borne up and sustained in our loneliness by the prayers and concern of our brothers all over the world. I shall never forget my old father's words during his last visit to me in the Gestapo office at the Oranienburg concentration camp. As he left he said, "My child, the Eskimos in Canada and the Bataks in Sumatra send you their greetings and are praying for you."'[2]

[1] The Churches Survey Their Task (London, 1937), p. 59.
[2] Christian News-Letter, March 20, 1946.

Light from dark days of the past may cheer us in days which seem as dark with threatening; days in which we acquiesce in the most dangerous division possible in the world; a division into two, with the nations grouped on either side of the 'Iron Curtain'. Perhaps there is not so much praying going on now by separated Christians for one another. If Russian Christians were to meet us, would they be likely to say that their coming together did not bring the experience of surprise, because they had already been so consciously close in prayer? Yet that is the sort of thing that might bring about a new creativity; and a genuine contact; for human divisions do not reach to Heaven.

What the eye does not see the heart does not grieve over. Those who feast at banquets – or who buy fish and chips at street corners – seldom think of the risks of the miner and the fishermen which their meal has made necessary. 'Most men would feel shame if caught preparing with their own hands precisely such a dinner, whether of animal or vegetable food, as is every day prepared for them by others,'[1] wrote Thoreau. Our trouble is not so much that we overwork our cooks as that we fail to realise the inevitable solidarity our needs create with a world of toiling and suffering men. We take it for granted that the tea shall be in the pot, the sugar in the bowl; without wondering very often what lives they live who gather tea-leaves in Ceylon, or cut sugar-cane in the West Indies. Western complacency has deeply affronted the nascent countries of Africa and Asia. The voice of Africa was heard in 1954 at the Evanston Assembly of the World Council of Churches, in the trenchant tones of Dr. Dagadu of the Gold Coast – which we must now learn to call Ghana:

'Many people outside Africa have been given the impression that the African is a lazy fellow, lying under a coco-nut or a banana tree, shaded from the tropical sun

[1] *Walden* (Everyman Edition), p. 190.

and waiting for the fruit to ripen and fall. Actually, Africans do all types of work, agricultural and industrial, where western methods have penetrated. . . . The world gets large quantities of the continent's rich gifts of gold, diamonds, copper and cocoa, due primarily to the industry of the Africans. The palm-oil and ground-nuts, from which we get much of our soap and cooking fats, the gold which you use to balance your national currencies, the cocoa for your morning breakfast, the rubber for your automobile tyres, and many other essential products come out of Africa principally through the labours of Africans.'

In the unified world of to-day, all those who so labour for us are our neighbours. What we have done, says Dr. Macleod, is to export our proletariat, while he argues that 'every Christian must be involved when we face the facts that a baby girl born in Canada can expect to live to the age of 69: born in India, the expectation is only 27 years; or that in Sweden infant deaths are 31.1 out of every thousand births, and in Gambia 369.'[1]

> *Thou shalt not kill, but needs not strive*
> *Officiously to keep alive*

wrote A. H. Clough sardonically. Already the population figures of eastern countries have been affected by better medical facilities and better dieting; by the shots of penicillin which annihilate the scourge of yaws; and by the insistent propaganda which slowly, and with many reverses, induces people to give up primitive and wasteful agricultural methods. In consequence increasing demands are being made on the world's food supplies. If the infant mortality rate in Africa and India approached that of Sweden the problem of feeding the world's population might appear almost insoluble. No wonder that Dr. Macleod also concludes that 'the only

[1] *Op. cit.*, p. 20.

conflict in which a Christian can now take part, without confusion of face, is the War on Want.'[1] There is needed an awakening to the demands of true community which is comparable to the awakening achieved by the incessant propaganda of the anti-slavery movement. No doubt slave-traders in plenty in the eighteenth century heard in English parish churches the Commandment *Thou shalt do no murder*, and responded, *Lord, have mercy upon us, and incline our hearts to keep this law*, without realising that the ventures they financed and from which they drew profits made them murderers. 'Taking all the deaths together – in the slave-catching wars or raids, on the march to the sea, during the "Middle Passage" and in "seasoning" – it has been moderately reckoned that for every African who became a "seasoned" slave at least one other African was killed.'[2]

Each age presents its particular challenge to the Christian Church. The last century was the great age of missionary expansion overseas; and its consequence is a series of Christian outposts which circle the world. Nor must the missionary endeavour cease. But it needs to be continually validated by evidence of a Church in action in obedience to Jesus Christ. As we have seen, this has been called the century of the refugee. There are calculated to be thirty millions of them in the world, and there are few countries without them. Their succour and support is a permanent obligation of a Church which prays *Give us this day our daily bread*. Through the Christian's reverence for life 'made in the image of God' he is obligated to save life. There are many

[1] *Ibid.*, p. 112.

[2] R. H. Coupland, *The British Anti-Slavery Movement* (London, 1933), p. 25.
The 'Middle Passage' was the voyage, often protracted, from Africa to the West Indies. It was reckoned in the later eighteenth century that on the average at least one-sixth of a cargo died on the voyage. 'The first four months of employment were known as the period of "seasoning", and during it no less on an average than one-third of the novices failed to adjust themselves in body or spirit to the new conditions of climate or food or labour, and died.'

means by which this is to be done. Inter-Church Aid represents one united agency of the non-Roman Churches through which they are learning to do together what they could never do alone; and through which they are experiencing a deeper unity in the service of the one Master. Christians who take their practical tasks seriously give the best testimony to the spiritual purpose by which they are motivated and the spiritual strength by which they are sustained. It was the Christian conscience which roused the world to the plight of the slaves: the Christian conscience needs to be so stung to concern for the world's forgotten people – languishing, as many of them do, in hutted camps, a prey to disease and to hopelessness – that the consciences of Christians will effectively stir the conscience of the world.

It is only recorded in one place that Jesus of Nazareth was angry. People were watching Him in the synagogue at Capernaum to see whether He would heal a man on the Sabbath day. 'And he saith unto the man that had his hand withered, Stand forth, And he saith unto them, Is it lawful on the sabbath day to do good, or to do harm? to save a life, or to kill? But they held their peace. And when he had looked round upon them with anger, being grieved at the hardening of their hearts, he saith unto the man, Stretch forth thy hand.'[1] The hardening of men's hearts is a condition endemic in human society. It were well for Christians to remember that this above all things brings grief to their Master; that it stirs Him to anger. And the parable of the great assize is a reminder that no excuses count with God. 'Inasmuch as ye did it not unto one of these least, ye did it not unto me.'[2]

Jesus came to save life. He came that men might have life and have it more abundantly. The quality of life He makes possible is totally different from the unadventurous and benevolent self-indulgence we call good living. It cannot be had on the cheap. 'If thy foot cause thee to stumble, cut it

[1] Mark 3, 3–5.   [2] Matt. 25. 45.

off: it is good for thee to enter into life halt, rather than having two feet to be cast into Gehenna.'[1]

Reverence for life as the gift of God must include reverence for one's own life. For those who do not believe that there is a God, suicide may seem a natural termination to an existence which appears no longer to be either useful or pleasureable. The Greeks, and many others, so regarded it. Pliny indeed regarded man as superior to the gods because he could kill himself. But once a man effectively believes that at death, though the body turn to dust, the spirit returns to God who gave it, any calculated suicide is excluded: it is a personal affront to the majesty of God. It is an interesting fact that the highest suicide rates are in countries like Sweden, where physical comfort is highly developed, rather than in ruder lands where people prize life because they have to struggle to preserve it. There is a high rate of suicide also, no doubt, in lands whose peoples are politically oppressed. In some countries people flee the world from a sense of uselessness; in others from desperation. President Masaryk said that to examine suicide is to look into the bottom of the modern soul. There were suicides in the past but 'suicidism' was a modern social ailment, associated in particular with great cities.[2] A recent medical authority has made the broad generalisation that '*the most important stimulus for suicide is the loss of the inner feeling of identity with any of the social groupings implicitly or explicitly recognised by the culture-pattern and society in which a person lives* – if you like, the subjective experience of "excommunication".'[3] The threat of suicide is always an appeal for help. When suicide has taken place, or when the attempt has failed, there

[1] Mark 9. 45.

[2] *Modern Man and Religion* (London, 1938), ch. 1.

[3] E. H. Strauss, D.M., D.Sc., F.R.C.P., Physician, Department of Psychological Medicine, St. Bartholomew's Hospital, London. *British Medical Journal*, October 6th, 1956, p. 819.

is a great need for understanding and sympathy by Christian people. The attitude of shocked surprise seldom brings healing. It were well to remember that the ultimate judgment belongs to God; and that He is the God and Father of our Lord Jesus Christ.

What are we to say about capital punishment and the widespread modern controversies concerning its use? It is interesting that the demand in Great Britain for its complete or virtual abolition, which, of course, is not new, has become powerful two hundred years after a time when the number of offences punishable by death was steadily mounting until it reached the appalling figure of two hundred. The pressure came from country gentlemen fearful for their property in a period when there was no efficient police force. Whenever – and it was frequently – there was some public panic the gallows were threatened for further offences. 'Not only were horse and sheep stealing and coining capital crimes, but stealing in a shop to the value of five shillings, and stealing anything privily from the person, were it only a handkerchief. But such was the illogical chaos of the law, that attempted murder was still very lightly punished, though to slit a man's nose was capital. The effect of increased legal severity in an age that was becoming more humane, was that juries often refused to convict a man for minor offences that would lead them to the scaffold. Moreover, it was easy for a criminal, by the help of a clever lawyer, to escape on purely technical grounds from the meshes of an antiquated and over elaborate procedure. Out of six thieves brought to trial, five might in one way or another get off, while the unlucky one was hanged.'[1]

It was the task of Victorian patience to unravel these legal tangles, while Victorian humanitarianism was reducing the number of crimes punishable by death. So late as 1831 a boy of nine was sentenced to death for breaking a shop window

[1] G. M. Trevelyan, English Social History (London, 1944), p. 348.

and stealing two pennyworth of paint – though he was re-
prieved as a result of public clamour.[1] 'The advance in
humanity', as Professor Trevelyan rightly states, 'far more
than the boasted advance in machinery, was the thing of
which the nineteenth century had best reason to be proud.'[2]
In the twentieth century it is hard to speak of advances in
humanity. We should not lightly forget the many deaths by
extermination in gas chambers, and by cruelty in concentration camps. But in the limited field of the penal system the
advance has been real. Indeed, Archbishop Temple could
write in 1941, 'If I were asked to point to any great achievement of the Church of England in the twentieth century so
far as it has gone, I should point without hesitation to the
reform of our penal administration. It cannot be entered in
the Official Year Book of any denomination. But most of the
work of the Church in done, not by ecclesiastical officials,
nor under the direction of ecclesiastical committees, but by
members of the Church who do the ordinary work of the
world in the inspiration of Christian faith and in a spirit
sustained by Christian prayer and worship.'[3]

The Old Testament was far from being as cruel as the
'bloody code' of English law in the eighteenth century. Yet
to modern controversy about capital punishment as much as
to modern controversy about pacifism, the Old Testament is
alien. 'Whoso sheddeth man's blood, by man shall his blood
be shed: *for in the image of God made he man.*' What the
Jewish Law interpreted as a sanction for the death penalty
would by many Christians to-day be taken as a sound
argument for its abolition. Though the murderer has failed
to reverence the life of his victim, his own life remains
important: it is still the gift of God, unique and irreplace-
able. He is still made in God's image: he is still a brother for

[1] George Godwin, *Crime and Social Action* (London, 1956), p. 101.
[2] *Op. cit.*, p. 508.
[3] *Citizen and Churchman* (London, 1941), p. 47.

whom Christ has died. Shall fallible human justice encroach upon the divine prerogative of vengeance? Moreover, the will of the community, which justice must respect, has become uncertain and wavering. It is not so very long since there were public executions in England – the last was on May 26th, 1868. They were appreciated as a public entertainment. Ghoulishness of this kind still exists; but it has been diverted into other channels. The rising tide against capital punishment is not mere sentimentalism. It is moved not only by sensitive feelings but by troubled consciences.

That the community has the right, in the last resort, and in self-defence, to take a man's life, only a minority would deny. It is, however, a growing feeling that this action should indeed be, in the last resort, a power held in reserve rather than one normally employed. Whether the death penalty is specially deterrent is continually debated. It is claimed that in none of those states which have abolished the death penalty – Argentina, Belgium, Brazil, Colombia, Costa Rica, Denmark, Ecuador, Finland, Holland, Portugal, Queensland (Australia), Sweden, Switzerland, Uruguay, and New Zealand – has there been any increase in the murder statistics.[1] Nothing could be more horrible than that an innocent man should be executed. That possibility remains. Moreover, the carrying out of an execution can have a demoralising effect upon a whole prison community; to say nothing of the hysteria which it enables the less responsible sections of the press to evoke in the less responsible sections of the public. There is no certain direction from the New Testament in this matter. But the New Testament promises that the Holy Spirit will guide with God's truth, in unprecedented situations, those whose trust is in God. It may be that in this area of our living the Holy Spirit is leading us to take new ventures and to make a new advance; and that the men of later ages, reading our history, will be amazed at our timidity

[1] Godwin, *op. cit.*, p. 194.

and insensitivity. Nevertheless there is still disagreement, even among those who do the ordinary work of the world in the inspiration of Christian faith and in a spirit sustained by Christian prayer and worship.

Jesus did not tell His followers that they should have no enemies; but He made the revolutionary suggestion that they should love them. Familiar words had already been written in the Book of Proverbs:

> If thine enemy be hungry, give him bread to eat;
> And if he be thirsty, give him water to drink:
> For thou shalt heap coals of fire upon his head,
> And the Lord shall reward thee.[1]

This might encourage a self-righteous appeal to God to reward a calculating benevolence. When St. Paul quotes these words he reaches a different conclusion: 'Be not overcome of evil, but overcome evil with good.'[2] The danger of resisting evil is always that of becoming evil. A Christian must always be aware of his own weakness and fallibility. 'But for the grace of God there goes John Bradford' – so declared a wise and courageous Christian as he saw some prisoners being led away to execution. When others are condemned it is well to ask why one has not oneself been condemned.

St. John went further than St. Paul:

> Whosoever hateth his brother is a murderer: and ye know that no murderer hath eternal life abiding in him.[3]

He could make this startling pronouncement because of an experience of new life and of grace common to all Christians. Murder is the denial of life; and so is hatred. Those whose lives are made by Christ and depend upon His grace are linked in a community of love. They are not to rest content until they make that community co-extensive with humanity itself.

---

[1] Prov. 25. 21, 22.   [2] Rom. 12. 20.

[3] 1. John 3. 15.

VII

THE SANCTITY OF MARRIAGE

Thou shalt not commit adultery. *Exodus 20. 14.*

And the Lord sent Nathan unto David. And he came unto him, and said unto him,

There were two men in one city; the one rich, and the other poor. The rich man had exceeding many flocks and herds: but the poor man had nothing, save one little ewe lamb, which he had bought and nourished up: and it grew up together with him, and with his children; it did eat of his own morsel, and drank of his own cup, and lay in his bosom, and was unto him as a daughter. And there came a traveller unto the rich man, and he spared to take of his own flock and of his own herd, to dress for the wayfaring man that was come unto him, but took the poor man's lamb, and dressed it for the man that was come to him. And David's anger was greatly kindled against the man; and he said to Nathan, As the Lord liveth, the man that done this is worthy to die: and he shall restore the lamb fourfold, because he did this thing, and because he had no pity.

And Nathan said to David, Thou are the man.

2. Samuel 12. 1–7.

Ye have heard that it was said, Thou shalt not commit adultery: but I say unto you, that every one that looketh on a woman to lust after her hath committed adultery already with her in his heart. *Matthew 5. 27, 28.*

Have ye not read, that he which made them from the beginning made them male and female, and said, For this cause shall a man leave his father and mother, and shall cleave to his wife; and the twain shall become one flesh? So that they are no more twain, but one flesh. What therefore God hath joined together, let not man put asunder. *Matthew 19. 4–6.*

The night is far spent, and the day is at hand: let us therefore cast off the works of darkness, and let us put on the armour of light. Let us walk honestly, as in the day; not in revelling and drunkenness, not in chambering and wantonness; not in strife and jealousy, but put ye on the Lord Jesus Christ, and make not provision for the flesh, to fulfil the lusts thereof.

Romans 13. 12–14.

Or know ye not that your body is a temple of the Holy Ghost which is in you, which ye have from God? and ye are not your own; for ye were bought with a price: glorify God therefore in your body. *1. Corinthians 6. 19–20.*

O Almighty God, who alone canst order the unruly wills and affections of sinful men; Grant unto thy people that they may love the thing which thou commandest, and desire that which thou dost promise; that so, among the sundry and manifold changes of the world, our hearts may surely there be fixed, where true joys are to be found; through Jesus Christ our Lord. Amen. *Collect for the Fourth Sunday after Easter.*

THOU shalt not commit adultery. The Ten Commandments come from a world of male domination. A man's wife – and he might have more than one – was regarded as his property. The greatest harm a man could do to another was to steal his wife from him. That remains true. But the relationship of the sexes can no longer be regarded as one of possessor and possessed. Christian insight, on the one hand, and, on the other, the emancipation of women – which owes more to Christianity than is always realised – have reinterpreted that relationship as one of mutual responsibility.

In the ancient world the position of women was usually a low and sometimes a degraded one. There were, of course exceptions. But the scrap of papyrus, containing the letter of a working man away from home in search of a job, which has been recovered from the sands of Egypt, and which bears a date which is equivalent to 1 B.C., indicates what must have been a common attitude. 'If – good luck to you! – you bear a child, if it is a boy, let it live; if it is a girl, expose it.'[1] The unwanted girl child would be left in the open to die, or to be taken away, if some kindly person were as kindly disposed towards an unwanted child as nowadays a kindly person might be to a stray kitten. An unknown second-century apologist for Christianity wrote of Christians: 'They marry like all other men and they beget children; but they do not cast away their offspring.'[2] One reason why the early Church grew was because it collected and cared for unwanted orphans of this kind. The Jews did not practise 'exposure' either: but the Jewish prayer book, to this day, reflects the old sense of male superiority:

> *Men say:*
> Blessed art thou, O Lord our God, King of the universe, who hast not made me a woman.
> *Women say;*
> Blessed art thou, O Lord our God, King of the universe, who hast made me according to thy will.[3]

Where Christianity has been newly introduced into a culture, its effect has been to raise the estimate in which women are held and to open for them many new possibilities. Often, however, one of the Christian missionary's most

[1] *Selections from the Greek Papyri*, edited G. Milligan (Cambridge, 1921), p. 33.

[2] *Ad Diognetum.* H. M. Gwatkin, *Selections from early Christian Writers* (London, 1911), p. 15.

[3] *The Authorised Daily Prayer Book of the United Hebrew Congregations of the British Empire* (15th edition, London, 1935), p. 6.

difficult tasks is to persuade men to allow their daughters to be educated, Ingrained prejudices die hardly. In parts of Africa one of the chief barriers to rapid Christian expansion has been the Christian demand for monogamy. In the Nigerian dioceses of the Anglican Communion, for example, men with more than one wife cannot be members of a Church Council. The official body, therefore, tends to be made up of younger men, while the more influential elders are excluded – to make their influence felt from the background. The demand for monogamy has also occasioned the breaking away from the Church of native African sects which make no such demand. The step from a world of Old Testament customs, or rather of customs below the standard of the Old Testament, to one in which the standard is set by the New is neither easily taken nor easily maintained.

Nor is it easy for the West. At one time the force of public opinion was markedly in favour of Christian moral standards. This support by convention occasioned much hypocrisy and much cruelty – for example, to unmarried mothers and their children – and it was a potent source of pharisaism. If the press is to be credited, in these days divorce is almost taken for granted among the film actors and actresses of Hollywood, California; but Gertrude Atherton has recorded the public attitude, in the same State, ninety years ago to her mother's divorce, which 'created a terrific sensation. In these days it is difficult to realize the disgrace involved by divorce in the 'sixties. It is possible that my mother was the first woman to apply for one in San Francisco. My grandfather and grandmother had the sympathy of the community. My father forswore drink for ever and devoted himself to business; Society knew him no more. My mother was ostracized as if she had been a leper wandering through the streets in a cowl, a warning bell in her hand.'[1]

These are more merciful days. But it is at peril that we

[1] *Adventures of a Novelist* (London, 1932), p. 16.

forget that monogamy is the great achievement of civilisation; an achievement which makes others possible. An English judge could remark in 1954: 'We have, I fear, unfortunately reached a position where adultery – or infidelity or misconduct as soft-hearted people call it – is considered to be a matter of little moment. It is no bar to advancement in any offices of the State, high or low, whereas any other form of stealing would mean the end of a career[1].' The weakness of to-day lies in an emphasis upon individual satisfaction to the disregard of corporate responsibility. 'Have ye not read, that he which made them from the beginning made them male and female, and said, For this cause shall a man leave his father and mother, and shall cleave to his wife; and the twain shall become one flesh? So they are no more twain, but one flesh. What therefore God hath joined together let not man put asunder.'[2] It is this sense of the two becoming one, of loyalty to a marriage which is not only entered into by mutual vows, but is itself a mutual achievement, that appears lacking to-day. 'The twain shall become one flesh' is very different from 'The two shall enjoy each other so long as they are suited, and then find a way out'; for if the achievement of unity has been real there is no way out which is not painful destruction of a precious creation. There is a sense indeed in which it can never be destroyed.

What is dangerous to marriage is any doctrine of limited liability. This is nowhere officially held. In English Registry Offices, for example, a notice reminds those assembled that according to law marriage is the lifelong union of one man to one woman. Unofficial attitudes are different; and this bald announcement may be as lightly regarded as the tables of the law painted in the east end of old-fashioned churches. In consequence the prospects of lifelong marriage are much less

[1] Mr. Justice Denning, May 2nd, 1954, quoted Archbishop Garbett, *World Problems of To-Day* (London, 1955), p. 38, n.

[2] Matt. 19. 4–6.

certain than they once were. In 1911 only two in every thousand marriages in England and Wales were terminated by divorce, in 1922 only eight. By 1937 it was sixteen, and by 1950 it had grown to seventy-one. In 1954 the number had fallen to sixty-seven. This increase is partly, of course, as the Royal Commission on Marriage and Divorce, from whose report these figures have been taken,[1] points out, because many people can now get a divorce who could not get one before. The complexities of modern life also multiply causes of disagreement, while the scarcity of houses prevents many young couples from starting their married life in a home of their own. 'Some of them then postpone having children, and this in itself can be a factor of marital disharmony. Moreover, people are marrying at an earlier age, when they may not be so apt to choose their partners wisely; statistics record a relatively high proportion of casualties in marriage where the wife married at a very early age.'[2]

But the basic problem is mental and spiritual, as the report does not hesitate to point out: 'There is a further factor in the problem of marriage breakdown, which is more dangerous, because more insidious in its effects, than any of the others. In fact, we believe it lies at the root of the problem. There is a tendency to take the duties and responsibilities of marriage less seriously than formerly. Yet if, as we have said, more is now asked of marriage, it follows that more, not less, should be put into it. The result of this outlook is that there is less disposition to overcome difficulties, and to put up with the rubs of daily life and, in consequence, there is an increasing disposition to regard divorce, not as the last resort, but as the obvious way out when things begin to go wrong. In other words, remedies which are intended for the relief of real hardship are used in cases where relief

[1] London, *Cmd. 9678*, p. 8, n, where the figures are given as percentages.

[2] *Ibid.*, para. 44.

should be unnecessary if a proper view of their marriage obligations were taken by husband and wife.'[1]

Modern life is not only complex; it also places great emphasis upon the physical in the relationship of the sexes. Young people are led to expect thrills and excitement continually. They want the best; and if, after a time, they seem no longer able to give each other the best, why should they not agree to seek it elsewhere? 'Our society', it has been said, 'is possessed and dominated in a quite remarkable way by the idea of passion. . . . In the person under its sway this notion of love becomes a vivid expression of egotism with its demands to possess and experience, its rejection of the two-in-oneness which bestows fulfilment and fruition on marriage. It is bound to lead to excessive concentration on the specifically sexual characteristics in both persons and relationships, and the exaltation of the external qualities stressed by the fictions and fashions of the hour, and the disparagement of fidelity. A marriage begun on the basis of these assumptions must, unless they are soon enlarged, be doomed to disappointment.'[2]

This is not new – indeed the report from which these words were taken was issued in 1943. The unruly wills and affections of sinful men have bedevilled life from the first, as the Bible bears abundant testimony – unruly affections as much as unruly wills. Behind the present mixture of romanticism and sensualism, however, there now lies the pressure of pictorial advertising, of newspapers and magazines reproduced in their millions, of the dance-halls with their two hundred million annual attendances, and the cinemas with their thirteen hundred million annual admissions.[3] The love-life of Hollywood may not be so debased as the movie

[1] *Ibid.*, para. 47.

[2] *Home and Family Life* (Report to the British Council of Churches London, 1943), p. 25.

[3] T. Cauter & J. S. Downham, *The Communication of Ideas*, A Study of Contemporary Influences on Urban Life (London, 1954), p. 134.

magazines suggest; but the fact that cinema heroes and heroines, who exercise so powerful an influence on adolescents, are publicised as taking marriage bonds very lightly, has succeeded in giving adultery a quite fashionable cachet. But it is not just adultery which is wrecking marriages to-day. It is the 'easy way out' which is provided by the introduction of desertion as a ground of divorce; and which in Britain has occasioned petitions on the ground of desertion amounting to nearly half the total number of divorce petititions presented.[1]

The cost of all this is seen in terms of children. The headmaster of a public school once told the author that the hardest job he had to do, and one that came round far too often was to tell a boy that his parents were about to start divorce proceedings. 'Each year in Great Britain some 20,000 children under the age of sixteen are affected by the divorce of their parents.'[2] In an address to the Annual Conference of the Association of Children's Officers, the Secretary of the National Marriage Guidance Council recently pointed out a great change which had taken place, which had been hardly noticed, or else taken for granted. There were still orphanages, but they were not being filled with orphans! 'The Victorians hoped through education, persuasion and moral enlightenment, to raise the social conduct of the nation; but thought that disease and premature death were to be accepted with resignation. In fact, it was the supposedly inevitable disasters that had been largely overcome. . . . The ancient threats to family life and the welfare of children, right through history until this century, arose mainly from bodily infirmity. Now they increasingly came from breakdowns in human relationships. They were social rather than medical in origin.' He calculated that of the 64,000 children in the care of local authorities in England and Wales, most

[1] Royal Commission, para. 139.
[2] *Ibid.*, para. 360.

of those who were there for other than quite short periods, were there because of some break-up of their homes for reasons other than their parents' illness or death.[1]

It is often claimed that it were better for children to endure the consequences of parental divorce than to live in an atmosphere of continual suspicion and recrimination. But social workers often reply that any real home is better than none at all. It is pointed out in the Royal Commission's Report that 'the best home for children is of course a happy home, but in our opinion (and most of our "expert" witnesses confirm this) children can put up with a good deal of friction between their parents so long as their home remains intact. The relations between the parents must be very bad indeed before a divorce is in the interests of the children.'[2]

It is frequently pleaded in extenuation of a lowered standard of sexual morality and a growth of promiscuity that 'after all it's only natural.' This was being said in the reign of the first Elizabeth, for in the Eleventh Homily it is remarked of adultery – defined as 'unlawful use of those parts, which be ordained for generation' – that 'this vice is grown unto such an height, that in a manner among many it is counted no sin at all, but rather a pastime, a dalliance; and but a touch of youth; not rebuked, but winked at; not punished, but laughed at.'' All this is indeed natural, provided that society is content with living at a level little removed from that of animals – we will not say, at a primitive level, for primitive societies possess their own customs and taboos by which the relationship of the sexes is regulated. Were man content to live at this merely 'natural' level, civilisation, as we have known it, would disappear; and there are plenty of warnings that a decay in sexual morality is an early sign of a civilisation's decline. Discipline, in this view, is not natural at all. Yet discipline is necessary for the

---

[1] *Marriage Guidance* (London), December, 1956.

[2] Para. 69 (iii), Views of nine members.

attainment of any worthy end, and for the acquiring of any form of proficiency – whether it be learning to drive a motor-car, learning a language, or learning to play a musical instrument.

It is a weakness of to-day that there appear to be fewer incentives for proficiency in living. The finest lives have usually been lived by those who have the clearest ideas about what life is for. In a state of uncertainty men and women will try any experiment and accept any easy gratification. Belief stands at the basis of any sound society; and where there is no belief the people cast off restraint. St. Paul could make a powerful appeal for sexual discipline when he wrote to the Corinthian Christians – men who had to reach a high standard in a notoriously immoral city – 'Know ye not that your body is a temple of the Holy Ghost, which is in you, which ye have from God? and ye are not your own; for ye were bought with a price: glorify therefore God in your body.'[1]

In the world of to-day the restraint of fear, which once was so powerful, is largely relaxed. Modern methods of birth control make it possible for all but the most inexpert to avoid giving birth to children. Without them the proportion of illegitimate children, and of children of doubtful paternity, would obviously be greatly increased. This means that the danger to society through adultery and fornication is greater than appears on the surface. The threat goes behind Christian belief and practice: it is a threat to civilisation itself. To quote Professor E. O. James: 'Promiscuity, fornication, adultery and all irregular sexuality are evil because they constitute a perverse use of a right impulse for wrong ends, namely the gratification of desire divorced from its legitimate purpose. The intense pleasure associated with the sex act is lawful and right within its proper context, notwithstanding the strictures placed upon it by some Christian

[1] 1. Cor. 6. 19, 20.

writers. To isolate it from creation and the sacramental
character and significance of the marriage relationship is an
abuse of the sex instinct, and in the case of adultery it has
disastrous consequences, inflicting a serious injury on the
other partner and the family. Furthermore, by bringing dis-
cord into the domestic group and making family life insecure it has a harmful effect on society. Therefore in all
states of culture restrictions, often in the form of stringent
taboos, have been enforced to prevent any irregularities
which would prove to be socially disturbing and injurious.'[1]

From their experiences at Sinai the desert tribes went forward to the slow conquest of the promised land. It was not
so easy a process as has sometimes been imagined; and it was
much more prolonged. It was only in David's time that
Jerusalem was taken from the Jebusites. There was much
sporadic conflict, much give and take, much inter-marriage.
'And the children of Israel dwelt among the Canaanites; the
Hittite, and the Amorite, and the Perizzite, and the Hivite,
and the Jebusite: and they took their daughters to be their
wives, and gave their own daughters to be their wives, and
served their gods.'[2] This inter-marriage is always to be
expected when there are armies of occupation. In this instance, also, the stranger within the gates presented not only
an opportunity for charity but an incitement to idolatry.
Moreover, the dice were loaded against those who came in
from the desert. 'The Lord thy God bringeth thee into a
good land, a land of brooks of water, of fountains and depths
springing forth in valleys and hills; a land of wheat and
barley, and vines and fig trees and pomegranates; a land of
oil olives and honey . . .'[3] Here was all the richness of a brave
new world, doubly attractive for those who came from the
austerities of desert life. But its attractiveness, combined

[1] *Marriage and Society* (London, 1952), p. 151.
[2] Judges 3. 5, 6.
[3] Deut. 8. 7, 8.

with their inexperience, made it also doubly dangerous. The Israelites had not grown vines, or figs, or olives before. They had now to learn agriculture and arboriculture; to learn from Canaanites, Amorites and Jebusites. As they learned these skills they learned also the religious practices which went with them; practices which no good farmer should neglect. So, from the disciplined life of the desert they turned to the 'natural' life of cultivated lands. They propitiated the local baals, or supernatural owners of the land: they joined in the feasts at the local shrines: they might remember the God of Sinai; but even as they did so they treated Him as if He were also the god of some fertility cult, a baal like all the rest.

In the feasts of the fertility cults drunkenness and sexual immorality both had their part. The high places, as the shrines were named, had their sacred prostitutes. To this whole cultus the canonical prophets were opposed, though many of those whom the Bible names 'false prophets' gave it their support. The opposition appears most clearly in the pages of Hosea, who insisted that these practices destroyed men's thinking powers. 'Whoredom and wine and new wine take away the understanding.'[1] No wonder that die-hards wanted to have nothing to do with the new civilisation but to reproduce the conditions of the desert; that even Hosea could picture God enticing His people into the wilderness again that He might woo her afresh as a bride.[2] Yet the prophets knew that for the nation there was no way back. They must find God in the present and in the future as they had found Him in the past. That remains true for the twentieth century. There can be no return to Victorian restrictions. The way must be forward; not to an unrestricted future, but to one in which Christians accept the discipline that is right for the situation. All discipline involves cost. But a Christian's discipline is always marked with a

[1] Hosea 4. 11.   [2] Hosea 2. 14.

cross. That may make it doubly costly, but it will also make it doubly creative.

The thought of Jesus of Nazareth was in some ways akin to that of Hosea. He also recognised that sensualism was a barrier to clarity of thought – to that process of fundamental re-thinking which was essential to repentance. An evil and adulterous generation kept seeking signs; wanting some extra authentication which was not sufficiently provided by His presence. His words and His acts.[1] An adulterous person is inevitably insecure. He turns from the proper security of home to passing experiences of security outside. The Jewish people in the time of Jesus thought they were secure. But few of them felt really free in their Father's house: they were worried by the feeling that there were laws that they should be keeping, unrealised laws, also, which they might be continually breaking. So they wanted signs. An appetite for sensation also demands ever greater sensations: if signs on earth are not convincing, cannot there be signs from heaven? The sensualist becomes easily sentimental; but he hurries from any summons to critical thought. Nevertheless Jesus showed great tenderness to those who were the victims of men's unregulated appetites. When the Pharisees brought before Him a woman who had been caught in the very act of adultery, they inquired what they should do. Moses had commanded stoning as a suitable punishment: what did Jesus say? For a long time He said nothing, but occupied Himself with making marks on the ground. Then He said, 'He that is without sin among you, let him first cast a stone at her.' And gradually they all went out; until Jesus was left with the woman alone. Then, at last, He looked her in the eyes. 'Woman, where are they? did no man condemn thee? And she said, No man, Lord. And Jesus said, Neither do I condemn thee: go thy way: from henceforth sin no more.'[2]

[1] Matt. 12. 39, 16. 4. Cf. Mark 8. 38.
[2] John 8. 8–11.

Nor was this instance an isolated one. Jesus was widely condemned for consorting with the riff-raff of the population. Was He not followed around by Mary of Magdala 'from whom seven devils had gone out'?[1] People could not understand why He preferred the company of tax collectors of doubtful loyalty, and others of doubtful morality, to their own. Nor could they make it out when He told His critics 'the publicans and the harlots go into the kingdom of God before you.'[2] Self-esteem can blind men's sight and obscure their thinking quite as much as sensuality.

The really startling thing that Jesus did was to trace the adulterous act to its origin in the sinful desire, and to condemn it there. 'From within, out of the heart of man, evil thoughts proceed, fornications, thefts, murders, adulteries, covetings. . . .'[3] And in the Sermon on the Mount He declared: 'Ye have heard that it was said, Thou shalt not commit adultery: but I say unto you that every one that looketh upon a woman to lust after her hath committed adultery with her already in his heart.'[4] By this standard we are all condemned; and our hoardings and picture papers and shiny magazines appear as panders to an adulterous generation. Few have the determination to apply, even figuratively, the remedy which the Sermon on the Mount prescribes: 'And if thy right eye cause thee to stumble, pluck it out, and cast it from thee: for it is profitable for thee that one of thy members should perish, and not thy whole body be cast into hell.'[5] Yet the weakest can turn to that expulsive power of a new affection prescribed by St. Paul, when he wrote, 'whatsoever things are honourable, just, pure, lovely, of good report . . . think on these things.' A verse earlier he had written of the peace of God standing sentry over men's hearts and thoughts, guarding their emotions as well as their intellects.[6]

[1] Luke 8. 2.	[2] Matt. 21. 31.	[3] Mark 7. 21, 22.
[4] Matt. 5. 28.	[5] Matt. 5. 29.	[6] Phil. 4. 8 & 7.

The teaching of Jesus about divorce has occasioned much discussion and much dispute. In more than one passage He condemned divorce completely. In one passage in St. Matthew, an exception is allowed, 'except for fornication.'[1] Most scholars believe that this does not belong to the original saying, a conclusion 'confirmed by the fact that there was never any tradition in the early Church approving divorce for adultery.'[2] Yet if this be granted, the question still remains, how are we to employ His prohibition, especially in a society which is not composed, except in a small proportion, of convinced Christians? What is to be said, for example, to people like the late Sir Josiah Wedgwood, who condemned illiberal divorce legislation as 'not only idiotic but wicked, creating immorality and encouraging dishonesty'? May no mistakes be rectified?

The question is often asked whether Jesus, who did not legislate on any other matters, chose to do so on this. The reply, in the belief and practice of different Christian communions, and of different peiple within those communions, has varied. The Church of England, for example, is far more concerned about re-marriage after divorce than with the fact of divorce itself. What Jesus certainly did was to state the essential nature of marriage, that it is permanent, that its permanence rests in the two becoming one flesh. He admitted that Moses made exceptions 'for the hardness of their hearts.' And men's hearts are no less hard – though some would prefer to say soft – in our days than in the days of Moses. We have to see the words of Jesus in relationship to His whole attitude; in relation to His tenderness to those who had fallen by the way *and were repentant*, as well as to sternness to those who caused little ones to stumble. Would He approve Church societies whose rules would exclude the Magdalene from their membership?

[1] Matt. 19. 9.
[2] Lindsay Dewar, *New Testament Ethics* (London, 1949) p. 95.

E

In our present society, with its high divorce rate, in which marriage tends to be regarded as no more than a civil contract, out of whose obligations a clever lawyer will always be able to extricate those who have been trapped, the question comes regularly before Christian ministers. Most would agree with a threefold programme. In the first place, a high ideal of marriage must be maintained. In the second place, understanding help must be given to those who have failed; help given by those who remember Christ's withering scorn of self-satisfied religious people. '*Being sinners ourselves,*' wrote the late Bishop St. Clair Donaldson, 'the treatment of brothers who have sinned a little more obviously than we have is to us desperately difficult; and we bungle and make grievous mistakes.'[1] There is no more costly exercise of time and anguish than in trying to give this help – too often to people to whom the Christian way of life is strange, the Christian standard pitched far too high, and the Christian Good News only beginning to be relevant. In the third place, there must be a continual campaign of education for responsible marriage, beginning early and continuing late; and an insistence that it 'is not by any to be enterprised, nor taken in hand, unadvisedly, lightly or wantonly; but reverently, discreetly, soberly, and in the fear of God, duly considering the causes for which matrimony was ordained.'

Thou shalt not . . . A negative command fails at this point; indeed, all commands are insufficient. What the Christian Gospel promises is not knowledge of the right only, but power to do it; that He who was in all points tempted like as we are, yet without sin, will give us His power. If there is plenty of evidence in society of the tragedies caused by broken marriages, there is evidence also of the transforming power of Christian grace – not the grace of Christians, but the grace of their Lord. Those whose lives are themselves transformed are enabled to bring a transforming power to

[1] *Meditation on the Acts* (London, 1937), p. 71.

others. Nor are they overwhelmed by trage
know that God sent not His Son into the world to
the world, but that the world through Him might be
From His Cross Jesus looked upon the men of an adulte.
and sinful generation. Nevertheless He prayed, *Fathe*
forgive them, for they know not what they do.

VIII

REVERENCE FOR JUSTICE

Thou shalt not steal. *Exodus 20. 15.*

And he that stealeth a man, and selleth him, or if he be found in his hand, he shall surely be put to death. *Exodus 21. 16.*

He also that is slack in his work
Is brother to him that is a destroyer. *Proverbs 18. 9.*

When thou reapest thine harvest in thy field, and has forgot a sheaf in the field, thou shalt not go again to fetch it: it shall be for the stranger, for the fatherless, and for the widow: that the Lord thy God may bless thee in all the work of thine hands. When thou beatest thine olive tree, thou shalt not go over the boughs again: it shall be for the stranger, for the fatherless, and for the widow. When thou gatherest the grapes of thy vineyard, thou shalt not glean it after thee: it shall be for the stranger, for the fatherless, and for the widow.

And thou shalt remember that thou wast a bondman in the land of Egypt: therefore I command thee to do this thing.
Deuteronomy 24. 19–22.

Lay not up for yourselves treasures upon the earth, where moth and rust doth consume, and where thieves break through and steal: but lay up for yourselves treasures in heaven, where neither moth nor rust doth consume, and where thieves do not break through nor steal: for where thy treasure is, there will thy heart be also. *Matthew 6, 19–22.*

Give, and it shall be given unto you; good measure, pressed down, shaken together, running over, shall they give into your bosom. For with what measure ye mete it shall be measured to you again. *Luke 6. 38.*

Let him that stole steal no more: but rather let him labour, working with his hands the things that is good, that he may have whereof to give to him that hath need. *Ephesians 5. 28.*

Then were there crucified with him two robbers, one on the right hand, and one on the left. *Matthew 27. 38.*

O God, the strength of all them that put their trust in thee, mercifully accept our prayers; and because through the weakness of our mortal nature we can do no good thing without thee, grant us the help of thy grace, that in keeping of thy commandments we may please thee, both in will and deed; through Jesus Christ our Lord. Amen.

Collect for the First Sunday after Trinity.

THOU shalt not steal. The command was given to a migrant people, whose corporate wealth was small and whose individual possessions were few. Their very paucity made them the more treasured, the more carefully protected; for should they be stolen in the wilderness they could not be replaced. (In the world of to-day few possessions are more closely guarded than the pitiable parcels carried by refugees.) In the most primitive societies some fundamental honesty is essential, otherwise they will disintegrate into anarchy. The command *Thou shalt not steal* can be understood in the nursery; yet it has significance for those who work in the most complicated commercial enterprises or adopt the most sophisticated code of manners.

In human history the prohibition of theft has never proved effective for very long unless it has been backed by the sanction of force. In the days of settlement in the promised land, when the leadership of those whom the Bible calls judges was uncertain and sporadic, when 'every man did that which was right in his own eyes,'[1] life itself became insecure, and men clamoured for the permanent authority of a king. Remove the police from modern states and very soon law and order will collapse; unless some group of popularly supported *vigilantes* supply the lack and see to it that the community's will is obeyed. Unfortunately there have been few police about when Western people have made their first contact with non-Europeans, strangers to their civilisation; and the contemptuous bargains which have been struck, the mean trickery which has been employed, constitute some of the most flagrant denials of the Eighth Commandment, and remain the white man's shame. Glittering trash has been exchanged for marketable goods: alcohol has been used to make trickery more easy. The bitter cry of primitive peoples that their lands have been taken from them sounds through the history of all colonial powers; and not every primitive people has been able to find so eloquent and courageous a champion as have the Hereros of South-West Africa in the Rev. Michael Scott.

Examples of this are familiar to those who have even a nodding acquaintance with the literature of colonial expansion. Two come easily to hand. The first is from R. M. Ballantyne's *Hudson Bay*, which is still re-printed as a children's adventure book. He is describing an incident in the savage rivalry between the North-West Company and the Hudson's Bay Company for the fur trade of what is now Western Canada. The Hudson's Bay Company's look-out 'reported that he had discovered tracks of Indians in the snow, and that he thought they had just returned from a hunting expedition. No sooner was this heard than a grand ball was given to the North-West Company. Great preparations were made. . . . The evening came, and with it the guests; and soon might be heard within the fort sounds of merriment and revelry. . . . Without the gates, however, a

[1] Judges 17. 6 & 21. 25.

very different scene met the eye. Down in a hollow . . . a knot of men might be seen, muffled in their leathern coats and fur caps, hurrying to and fro with bundles on their backs and snow-shoes under their arms, packing and tying them firmly on trains of dog-sleighs. . . . Late on the following day the Nor'-West scouts reported the party of Indians, and soon a set of sleighs departed from the fort with loudly-ringing bells. After a day's march of forty miles, they reached the encampment, where they found all the Indians dead drunk, and not a skin, not even the remnant of a musquash, left to repay them for their trouble.'[1] In due course revenge followed; and upon this occasion it was the Hudson's Bay officers who were intoxicated while the Nor'-Westers got the furs. It is no wonder that the first English clergyman sent into the district in a courageous report to the Hudson's Bay Company, which was his employer, deplored 'the free use of the Rum Keg, through the medium of which the Natives were excited to quarrels that often terminated in murders, while it demoralised the European and Canadian Servants to the most unprincipled and degraded character.'[2] He had great hopes of Christian education; but it needed to have behind it the strength of civil power.

The second example is from the German settlement of South-West Africa. 'A trader camps near a Herero village. To him are driven oxen which the Herero wish to sell. "How much do you want for the oxen?" says the trader. "Fifty pounds sterling," says the Herero. "Good," says the trader. "Here you have a coat valued at £20, trousers worth £10, and coffee and tobacco worth £20, that is in all £50." The Herero is satisfied.'[3] The tragedy for this particular people is that a show of better treatment, through the

[1] *Hudson Bay* (4th. edition, London, n.d.), pp. 63, 64.

[2] MS. Report 13 Dec., 1823), in library of Church Missionary Society.

[3] Quoted, Freda Troup, *In Face of Fear*, Michael Scott's Challenge to South Africa (London, 1950), p. 39.

mandatory system of the League of Nations and the later trusteeship scheme of the United Nations, has not proved effective in practice. Like so many other native peoples they are offered lands, but they are lands which the white man has rejected as not good enough, and lands which demand expensive irrigation. White people have a way of knowing what is best for other people – and what is best for themselves as an extract from the 1936 Report on its Mandate by the Government of South Africa makes clear:

'With his boring machines, irrigation works, railways, motor cars, and even aeroplanes, his scientific knowledge generally and his industry and enterprise in particular, the white man has already done a great deal to develop South-West Africa, and can do a great deal more. The non-Europeans in the Police Zone should share in the benefits of this development, but owing to the wild and unsettled lives they used to lead and which they have not yet given up, they still have to learn how to function as part of a settled community under civilized conditions.'[1]

No matter how primitive peoples are, they can tell when they are being despised; and in time they can tell when they are being cheated. And the best of all authorities warns any who bear the name of Christian, *Take heed that ye despise not one of these little ones*.

The command *Thou shalt not steal*, as the Rev. John Drewett has well pointed out, is based not so much upon a reverence for the right of ownership of property as upon a reverence for justice.[2] There have been many occasions when the property-owning classes have behaved to the property-less in ways which might be condemned as theft. Amos condemned the rich people of Samaria who 'sold the righteous for silver and the needy for a pair of shoes',[3] who

[1] Quoted *Ibid.*, p. 66.
[2] *The Ten Commandments in the 20th Century* (London, 1941), p. 56 ff.
[3] Amos 2. 6.

were so insistent upon their rights that they left the poor cold at night while they used the cloaks they had taken from them as pledges, to make themselves comfortable while they reclined before the very altar of God.[1] 'Forasmuch, therefore as ye trample upon the poor, and take exactions from him of wheat: ye have built houses of hewn stone, but ye shall not dwell in them; ye have planted vineyards, but ye shall not drink the wine thereof.'[2] Jesus took up the strain when He condemned those 'which devour widows' houses, and for a pretence make long prayers.'[3] In a land where there was much injustice and irregular profit-taking the effect of the visit of Jesus upon one capitalist was for him immediately to declare, 'Behold, Lord, the half of my goods I give to the poor; and if I have wrongly exacted aught of any man, I restore fourfold.'[4] It was not the loss of goods but the possession of goods which made it hard for a man to come near to God; for 'It is easier for a camel to go through a needle's eye, than for a rich man to enter into the kingdom of God.'[5] When Christians make careful preparations for a comfortable retirement they do well to remember that their Master called a man who acted in this way nothing short of a fool. 'I will pull down my barns and build greater; and there will I bestow all my corn and my goods. And I will say to my soul, Soul, thou hast much goods laid up for many years; take thine ease, eat, drink, and be merry. But God said unto him, Thou fool, this night is thy soul required of thee; and the things which thou hast prepared, whose shall they be? So is he that layeth up treasure for himself, and is not rich toward God.'[6]

The teaching of Jesus went further than that of the Old Testament, else the disciples would hardly have greeted His condemnation of the rich with the question 'Then who can

---

[1] Amos 2. 8.   [2] Amos 5. 11.
[3] Mark 12. 40.   [4] Luke 19. 8.
[5] Mark 10. 25.   [6] Luke 12. 16–21.

be saved?'[1] But much of it was a re-publication of old truth. The present writer recalls that when he was a small boy he enjoyed listening to Bunyan's *Pilgrim's Progress* read aloud to him. But there was one passage which he resented. It was where Christiana's boys were reprimanded for eating fruit which fell from branches which grew over the wall of an enclosed garden. For the sake of the allegory this had to be the devil's garden; but to a boy it seemed a very reasonable thing to do. And so it might have seemed to the author of Deuteronomy, who made particular provision for a generosity which was to remove the temptation to petty thieving: 'When thou reapest thine harvest in thy field, and hast forgot a sheaf in the field, thou shalt not go again to fetch it: it shall be for the stranger, for the fatherless, and for the widow: that the Lord thy God may bless thee in all the work of thine hands. When thou beatest thine olive tree, thou shalt not go over the boughs again: it shall be for the stranger, for the fatherless, and for the widow. When thou gatherest the grapes of thy vineyards, thou shalt not glean it after them: it shall be for the stranger, for the fatherless, and for the widow. And thou shalt remember that thou wast a bondman in the land of Egypt; therefore I command thee to do this thing.'[2] It is a pity that commercial civilisation cannot devise some equivalent for the ungleaned vineyard and the unbeaten olive tree – particularly in those multiple stores, whose open counters, where everything is set out in such abundance, and not always obviously well guarded, provide a continual temptation for those whose powers of moral resistance are not very strong.

The temptation to theft does not spring only from necessity but from laziness; indeed, it is closely linked with other sins which are forbidden in the Commandments, in particular with covetousness. The early Christian document called the *Didache*, or Teaching of the Twelve Apostles, gives

[1] Mark 10. 26.   [2] Deut. 24. 19–22.

this instruction, 'My child, be not a liar: for the lie guideth to theft: nor a lover of money, nor vainglorious: for from all these things thefts are begotten.'[1] St. Paul recognised from what doubtful antecedents came many of the Gentile converts in the Levantine churches, and wrote in the Epistle to the Ephesians, 'Let him that stole steal no more: but rather let him labour, working with his hands the thing that is good, that he may have whereof to give to him that hath need.'[2] Here, wrote Dr. Armitage Robinson, 'is a complete reversal of the moral attitude. Instead of taking what is another's, seek with the sweat of your brow to be in position to give to another what you have honestly made your own.'[3] The hands which have been used for stealing must now be used for working, that they may be used for giving. If this is the right antidote to thieving, the right antidote to close-fistedness is to be found in an imaginative generosity; the generosity of one who has put himself in the other's place and begun to feel as he feels. And if Christianity is in any sense an imitation of Christ it is an imitation of the greatest generosity in all history. No one who has said from his heart, 'Thanks be to God for his unspeakable gift'[4] can straight away be niggardly. Yet the hold of things human is not easily shaken off. It seems so natural to be selfish. The Christian has constantly to be reminded of his Master's words: 'Lay not up for yourselves treasures upon the earth, where moth and rust doth consume, and where thieves break through and steal: but lay up for yourselves treasures in heaven, where neither moth nor rust doth consume, and where thieves do not break through nor steal: for where thy treasure is there shall thy heart be also.'[5]

There have been some Christians who have gone further

[1] 3. 5.
[2] 4. 28.
[3] *St. Paul's Epistle to the Ephesians* (London, 1903), p. 112.
[4] 2. Cor. 9. 10.
[5] Matt. 6. 19–21.

and tried to separate themselves from owning goods altogether. Francis of Assisi combined a following of Christ's
command to His disciples when they set out on their first
missionary journey to take nothing for the way, with obedience to the instruction given to the rich young man to sell
all that he had and give to the poor. Through this stern
obedience he gathered around him a group of devoted men
determined to go all the way with him. Through the same
obedience he initiated a great movement, both for the proclamation of the Gospel and the reclamation of decayed and
broken men and women. Through obedience he became a
saint. Completeness of renunciation gave him, as it has given
others, great spiritual authority. The Bishop of Assisi said to
him one day, 'Your way of living without owning anything
seems to me very harsh and difficult.' 'My lord,' replied
Francis, 'if we possessed property we should have need of
arms for its defence, for it is the source of quarrels and law-
suits, and the love of God and of one's neighbour usually
finds many obstacles therein.'[1] Many people think of him as
creating a mendicant order: that is not what he did; he
created a labouring order. It was the rich man's reformation
also to work with his hands the thing that is good.[2]

These examples are important. Without them Christian
life would be immeasurably the poorer. In the working world,
however, they cannot wholly be followed. When Jesus sent
out the disciples two by two, telling them to take nothing for
the journey, 'no scrip, no bread, no money in their purse: but
be shod with sandals, and put not on two coats,'[3] their faith
was being tested and their reliability in face of difficulty.
Such tests are devised nowadays by many youth organisa-
tions. The tour meant an intensification of the simplicity of

[1] Paul Sabatier, *Life of St. Francis of Assisi* (English tr. London,
1935), p. 80.

[2] *Ibid.*, p. 121.

[3] Mark 6. 7–9.

their daily lives. The very fact that they were told not to take things makes it clear that they possessed them; and would have taken them had they not been expressly forbidden. But this initial experience was one which they would never forget. It would affect their lives; their future attitude to material possessions. They would always remember what they had been able to get on without. In a money-loving age it would be well for more Christians to have experiences by which they learn to do without; by which they discover how few things are really necessary; so that a more Franciscan attitude towards possessions might mould the feelings and thinking of members of Christian congregations.

There have been few extensions of public ownership, however necessary, and however well compensated, which have not been attacked as daylight robbery. The necessary contributions which have to be made for national and local services are also deeply resented. It has been suggested that one reason why young men and women are once again emigrating from Great Britain to the Dominions is that they are sick of paying income-tax and buying insurance stamps. Man has always been a tax-resisting being. The achievement of the welfare state in Great Britain has produced so great a mass of regulations that a contempt for law has been engendered and has spread. So soon as a regulation is promulgated people begin to think out how it can be evaded. Firms employ experts in tax-avoidance who are said to save them thousands of pounds each year. But what did they save the community? Rationing always produces its black market, in which more than a person has a right to receive is available at more than he ought to pay. With the many benefits which are now available from public bodies there is a danger of a kind of black market in welfare, or at least of people skilled to secure more benefits than they might properly be thought to deserve. With this has gone an increase in petty pilfering. All of which is to be noted by Christians; and resisted in themselves and in others. For the great experiment of the welfare state is not likely to succeed unless it be based on morality, and unless a fair proportion both of its agents and of those they serve are in touch with a source of power greater than their own. 'Ye are the salt of the earth, but if the salt have lost its savour wherewith shall it be salted?' The salt of the earth is needed to-day. Men who live by a high standard raise the standard of those who live by a low one. Though it is Gresham's law that bad money drives out good, there is a certain converse to this in moral affairs. When there are saints about people find it hard to behave meanly. If the Church is in any sense the body of Christ it should have that effect upon the society in which it lives.

The danger is that the extension of public ownership shall produce an increase of private irresponsibility – in particular about what is publicly owned. The individual conscience, which might be greatly disturbed by news of theft from a neighbour, is not so deeply moved because a large industrial organisation loses an appreciable amount of raw material through odd bits being 'knocked off' by employees and used for their own ends. Public libraries annually report an increasing number of thefts; and even so exalted an institution as the Bodleian Library at Oxford has joined in the chorus. These thefts are not committed by the criminal classes. What is at fault is a lack of moral sense, and an unresisted laziness on the part of ordinary people. In railway trains conduct sometimes is not short of hysterical. The *Manchester Guardian* in 1956 described the havoc caused in a railway train returning from Manchester to Liverpool after an important football match in the former city. Eight door windows were broken, five side windows smashed, fourteen pictures broken, two mirrors cracked, one whole door was missing, while another was damaged: several dozen electric-light bulbs had vanished; luggage racks had been pulled from the walls as though people had been swinging on them;

a number of seats were slashed, and there was a good deal of blood-staining in some of the compartments.[1] A cynic might remark that a good time appears to have been had by all: but what would a visitor from Africa have made of it – one of those ignorant Hereros, for example, who because of their wild and unsettled lives have still to learn to function as a settled community under civilised conditions?

Theft is both an evasion of responsibility and a denial of neighbourhood. In a society in which the childish lesson has not been learned 'to keep my hands from picking and stealing' as the Church of England Catechism has it, it is hard to live at an adult level, because people have to be so constantly on the watch and do not know whom they may trust. In the society of the world when, as in 'the scramble for Africa' the nations are ready to grab the best for themselves and give the less good to others, a long-term resentment is created whose results are still unforeseeable. There is an inevitable egalitarianism in the fundamentals of human life among those who dare to pray, 'Give us this day our daily bread.' In 1804, the committee of the newly-formed Church Missionary Society, seeking recruits for its African mission, declared, 'We desire to make Western Africa the best remuneration in our power for its manifold wrongs,' and the deaths of fifty-three missionaries in Sierra Leone in the succeeding two decades revealed the sincerity of the desire. To-day that 'remuneration' needs to be continually backed by material sacrifice; as it is, in part, by the granting of self-government to Ghana and Nigeria; and by the provisions of the Colombo plan. But the attitude of the British public seldom attains the level of the statesmen by which it is represented.

A responsible attitude is needed also to the people of the future. In Britain many acres of valuable land, which might have been used for agricultural purposes, are now covered with slag heaps and the tips around coal mines. This represents,

[1] *Manchester Guardian*, March 5, 1956.

in a sense, a theft from the future, as does all wasteful use of natural resources. In many countries the erosion of the soil is a process which has been encouraged by spendthrift agriculture. There was a time when landowners planted trees so that their grandchildren might have the timber, a form of confidence in the future which does not come easily to a generation which looks for quick results. Something like this, however, needs to be the attitude, not so much of individual landowners, who are dwindling in numbers, but of those who guard the interests of the community. This is certain to arouse opposition. Nowadays people in the United States look back with gratitude on the decisions made by Theodore Roosevelt in 1907 by which the area of the national forests was increased from forty-three to a hundred and ninety-four million acres, and their wasteful use restrained; but, at the time, no policy of the administration excited sharper opposition than the President's efforts on behalf of conservation.[1]

Bishop Gore summarised five ways in which, apart from stealing in the ordinary sense, the commandment *Thou shalt not steal* is broken. This was part of his re-interpretation of the Commandments in the light of Christian belief. The five ways were as follows:

(1) By fraudulent dealings in business or trade, whereby our fellow-man receives for money, given something less, or other, than he had a right to expect.

(2) By 'sweating' or requiring others to work for inadequate wages.

(3) By giving or receiving bribes or, in other ways, defrauding an employer of the best service of the employed.

(4) By expecting others to work for us without doing our own fair share of work.

(5) By neglecting or inadequately performing the duty of almsgiving.[2]

[1] *Encyclopaedia Britannica.*   [2] *Op. cit.*, p. 212.

In respect to the last, it is well to remember that the Jewish people in the time of our Lord paid a tax of ten per cent for the support of their Church, while almsgiving was in addition to this. Too many people nowadays regard gifts to the Church as a form of charity. For the Church member it is nothing of the sort. It is taking your share in maintaining the society to which you belong. Generosity goes beyond this.

'Not slothful in business, fervent in spirit, serving the Lord':[1] St. Paul's words have been interpreted in ways which would have surprised their author; in particular, perhaps, by those Calvinistic business men who provided the backbone for the development of modern commercial enterprise. 'To the Puritan,' writes Professor Tawney,'a contemner of the vain shows of sacramentalism, mundane toil becomes a sort of sacrament.'[2] To the outsider the service of self has often seemed curiously intertwined with the service of the Lord; and even the nineteenth-century philanthropists, who gave to good causes with such unbounded generosity, do not always appear to have been so interested in the bodily welfare of those whose labours contributed so largely to their wealth as they were to their souls. It is always easy for a present generation to perceive and condemn the injustices and insensitiveness of those which have preceded it. We could do with some men like the banker Henry Thornton, who used his income from 1790 to 1793 as follows:

1790 Charity £2,260	All other expenses	£1,543
1791 £3,960		£1,817
1792 £7,508		£1,616
1793 £6,680		£1,988[3]

Taxation would make such a balance sheet impossible in

[1] Rom. 12. 11. (Authorised Version).

[2] *Religion and the Rise of Capitalism* (London, 1926), p. 199.

[3] Quoted, G. R. Balleine, *A History of the Evangelical Party in the Church of England* (London, 1908), p. 149.

Great Britain to-day. But in changed circumstances a great example can still be followed.

In the world of to-day enterprises grow larger and are more and more publicly owned or maintained. As more people become servants of the public the need for responsibility in services increases. Many public officials, in positions high and low, demonstrate that sacrificial service can be called forth by a statutory body as much as by a voluntary organisation. How great a debt modern Britain owes, for example, to its probation officers. What is needed to-day in particular is an increase in responsibility at the receiving end; a common readiness to work harder for the sake of the community. If this is to be achieved very many old patterns of thought and imagination will have to be dissolved, old fears assuaged. This will not be achieved by exhortation but through experience; through the shared experience of those who seek a common objective. This is achieved, in some industries, as in much scientific research, through the development of team-working. From these experiments others have probably much to learn. The society will not live in the modern world in which every man does that which is right in his own eyes. Nor would a society be strong in which everybody did what he was told to do. What is needed is a peaceful equivalent of Cromwell's soldiers who knew what they were fighting for and loved what they knew.

In the end a Christian has to remember that his life on earth is short; that his goods are held only in leasehold tenancy. He is appointed a steward; and he will have to give an account of his stewardship. The One to whom he is responsible, the One under whose judgment he stands, is the almighty and all-generous God.

IX

TELLING THE TRUTH

Thou shalt not bear false witness against thy neighbour.
Exodus 20. 16.

Thou shalt not go up and down as a talebearer among thy people. . . . I am the Lord. *Leviticus 19. 16.*

Lord, who shall dwell in thy tabernacle: or who shall rest upon thy holy hills?
Even he, that leadeth an uncorrupt life: and doeth the thing which is right, and speaketh the truth from his heart.
He that hath used no deceit in his tongue, nor done evil to his neighbour: and hath not slandered his neighbour. *Psalm 15. 1–3.*

But lo, thou requirest truth in the inward parts. *Psalm 51. 6.*

If any man thinketh himself to be religious, while he bridleth not his tongue but deceiveth his heart, this man's religion is vain. *James 1. 26.*

But what think ye? A man had two sons; and he came to the first, and said, Son, go work to-day in the vineyard. And he answered and said, I will not: but afterwards he repented himself and went. And he came to the second, and said likewise. And he answered and said, I go, sir: and went not. Whether of the twain did the will of his father? They say, The first. *Matthew 21. 28–31.*

Speaking truth in love. *Ephesians 4. 15.*

Let us hold fast the confession of our hope that it waver not; for he is faithful that promised. *Hebrews 10. 23.*

Faithful is he that calleth you, who will also do it.

1. Thessalonians 5. 24.

Almighty God, unto whom all hearts be open, all desires known, and from whom no secrets are hid: Cleanse the thoughts of our hearts by the inspiration of thy Holy Spirit, that we may perfectly love thee, and worthily magnify thy holy name; through Christ our Lord. Amen. *The Collect in the Communion Service.*

---

*T*HOU *shalt not bear false witness against thy neighbour.* Without true witness justice is impossible and the whole structure of law collapses. There is, no doubt, perjury enough in modern law-courts: not all witnesses tell the truth; not all tell the whole truth; and not all tell nothing but the truth. But what if perjury were to be expected as a matter of course? Civilised life would be in danger.

The Ninth Commandment was specially important for the Jews because Law meant more to them than it does to most of us. For them it was no mere necessary code, a book of rules which could be disregarded so long as life went smoothly useful in the background, but rarely though about. The Jewish ideal was the opposite of this.

> *Thy statutes have been my songs*
> *In the house of my pilgrimage*[1]

was the experience of many a scribe. Jewish religion thinks continually of the Law, or *Torah*. It is their way of life. Contrasts which seem natural to a Christian are strange to a Jew. 'The Rabbis declared that the Prophets were Torah, the Psalms were Torah; indeed, the whole Bible was Torah.'[2] God was the supreme Lawgiver. The lie was a

[1] Psalm 119. 54.

[2] C. G. Montefiore in *Record and Revelation* (Oxford, 1938), p. 435.

fundamental denial of His position and His rights. One rabbi has said, 'Everything in the world God created, except the art of lying. That is man's invention.'[1] If that be so, we live increasingly in a man-made world. Lord Coleraine has written that 'the danger which threatens us to-day does not come from an aggressive Germany. It does not even come from an aggressive Russia, though Russia may prove to be the vessel which carries it. It comes rather from the power of the lie in the modern world. The lie has commonly been accepted as a political instrument; there is nothing new in that. What is new is that in our day it is so thinly disguised, and so widely believed.'[2] It is because perjury is so often to be expected, almost as a matter of course, in international relationships, that civilised life is indeed in danger.

Thou shalt not bear false witness *against thy neighbour*. The modern world hardly regards truth as a denial of God's sovereignty. It recognises, however, that it is essentially un-neighbourly. Theft from another is refusal to be a neighbour: stealing a man's good name is a worse refusal:

> *Good name in man or woman, dear my Lord*
> *Is the immediate jewel of their souls;*
> *Who steals my purse steals trash; 'tis something, nothing;*
> *'Twas mine, 'tis his, and has been slave to thousands!*
> *But he that filches from me my good name*
> *Robs me of that which not enriches him,*
> *And makes me poor indeed.*[3]

Yet this is a form of theft which unregenerate men enjoy, and some who think they are regenerate. Perhaps Shakespeare was wrong in saying that the thief is not enriched by it. He gains, for the time being, a spurious sense of power. When a man's position appears impregnable you can at least express

[1] Goldman, *op. cit.*, p. 184.

[2] Richard Law, *Return from Utopia* (London, 1950), p. 31.

[3] Shakespeare, *Othello*, III, iii, 155.

your envy by calling him names; and in doing so share with others a feeling of being superior to him. And how easily lasting harm can be done by this malicious fellowship. It may be enough to say, 'Well, there's no smoke without fire' — a statement which has been called the tale-bearer's charter. The Marcan version of our Lord's list of the evil things which proceed from within and defile a man includes 'an evil eye.'[1] This has been variously interpreted, and might more naturally be linked with the commandment which forbids coveting. But one form of the evil eye which does great harm in society is the eye of suspicion; the eye which half sees, linked with the mind which moves rapidly to the worst possible conclusion, which in turn instigates the unbridled tongue. In human relations, as in the relationship of men with God, 'The lamp of the body is the eye: if therefore thine eye be single, thy whole body shall be full of light. But if thine eye be evil, thy whole body shall be full of darkness. If therefore the light that is in thee be darkness, how great is that darkness!'[2]

It were well for us sometimes to ponder the miracle of speech, which distinguishes human beings from the animal creation, which can only growl, bark, neigh, hiss, coo and twitter. Language is the essential means of communication between human beings, expressing an extensive range of emotions and making them more real through their expression. It becomes power on the lips of the orator, precision in the explanations of the scientist, music in the writings of the poet. Speech was followed by writing, which gave it new precision, fresh subtleties of expression and greatly extended powers of influence. After many millenia came the new power of printing, which helped to make the modern world. The Reformation, for example, owes very much to printing. The earlier movement of Lollardism in England could be stamped out: its translated Bibles were all of them manu-

[1] Mark 7. 22.   [2] Matt. 6. 22, 23.

scripts, laboriously copied by hand. If they were not actually destroyed, they could at least be driven into hiding. The situation was different when Tyndale's printed New Testaments began to seep into the country from the Continent. They could be destroyed; but others followed them. Printing indeed destroys the pretensions of any dominating Church. It has only failed to destroy the pretensions of totalitarian régimes because it has been met by a rigid censorship, mercilessly enforced. With improved techniques printing became even more powerful in the nineteenth century, as more people learned to read and more languages were reduced to writing. It raised many high hopes; so that in 1870 R. W. Emerson could write of 'the diffusion of knowledge, overrunning all the old barriers of caste, and, by the cheap press, bringing the university to every poor man's door in the newsboy's basket.'[1]

Unfortunately it is no longer the university of which we are prompted to think when we consider the cheap press. In the newspapers with the widest circulation to-day illustrations displace letterpress while circulation is maintained at fantastically high levels as much by the evasion of news as by its presence. It is little comfort that Britain is the world's greatest newspaper-reading country when we consider the kind of newspapers most of its inhabitants read. Sometimes one is tempted to parody St. Paul and suggest that whatsoever things are untrue, whatsoever things are dishonest, whatsoever things are unjust, whatsoever things are impure, whatsoever things are of ill report, these are what we are invited to consider.

Printing was followed by the telegraph and the telephone; then by the cinema, radio and television; and in consequence of this those who live a public life to-day do so before a changing public of millions, most of whom are more interested in some 'personal angle' to their lives than the

[1] *Society and Solitude*, ch. 2, Civilization.

policies they commend, the works they create, or the achievements by which they would wish to be judged. Meanwhile the sense of importance attached to printed or written words has been so diminished that many people are content to 'sign on the dotted line' where officials bid them, without having so much as glanced at the documents to which their signature is being attached. We are often told that oil is the prime need of our modern industrial civilisation. But where should we be if supplies of paper were withheld?

This is how Mr. Lewis Mumford writes of modern city life: 'As the day's routine proceeds the pile of paper mounts higher: the trashbaskets are filled and emptied and filled again. The ticker tape exudes its quotations of stocks and its reports of news; the students in the schools and universities fill their notebooks, digest and disgorge the contents of books, as the silkworm feeds on mulberry leaves and manufactures its cocoon, unravelling themselves on examination day. Buildings rise recklessly, often in disregard of ultimate profits, in order to provide an excuse for paper capitalizations and paper rents. In the theatre, in literature, in music, in business, reputations are made – on paper. The scholar with his degrees and publications, the actress with her newspaper clippings and the financier with his shares and voting proxies, measure their power and importance by the amount of paper they can command. No wonder the anarchists once invented the grim phrase: "Incinerate the documents!" That would ruin the world quicker than universal flood and earthquake.'[1]

All this is an invitation to irresponsibility. Men were more careful what they wrote when all they had available was a comparatively expensive papyrus roll or skin of vellum. It is hard to feel the same about newsprint, which to-day is, and to-morrow is used to light the fire. Yet responsibility is even more important, for the newsprint reaches millions of

[1] *The Culture of Cities* (London, 1940), p. 257.

homes. Taking God's name in vain, as we have seen, breaks the covenant between man and God: false witness against a neighbour breaks the covenant between man and man. The use of speech is always an attempted exercise of power, to persuade, inform, entertain, encourage or depress, enlighten or deceive. Of its dangers St. James, among biblical writers, was particularly aware:

'We all make mistakes in all kinds of ways, but the man who can claim that he never says the wrong thing can consider himself perfect, for if he can control his tongue he can control every other part of his personality! Men control the movements of a large animal like the horse with a tiny bit placed in its mouth. And in the case of ships, for all their size and the momentum they have with a strong wind behind them, a very small rudder controls their course according to the helmsman's wishes. The human tongue is physically small, but what tremendous effects it can boast of! A whole forest can be set ablaze by a tiny spark of fire, and the tongue is as dangerous as any fire with vast potentialities for evil. It can poison the whole body, it can make the whole of life a blazing hell.

'Beasts, birds, reptiles and all kinds of sea-creatures can be, and in fact are, tamed by man, but no one can tame the human tongue. It is an evil always liable to break out, and the poison it spreads is deadly. We use the tongue to bless our Father, God, and we use the same tongue to curse our fellowmen, who are created in God's likeness. Blessing and curses come out of the same mouth – surely, my brothers, this is the sort of thing that never ought to happen.'[1]

The despair of this passage will be shared by those who have suddenly been confronted with the consequences of their

[1] James 3. 2–10, tr. J. B. Phillips, *Letters to Young Churches* (London, 1947).

own irresponsible talk. *Careless talk costs lives* was a common war-time announcement. It is true at all times. We contribute to the social fabric of our community by the things we say and by the things we leave unsaid. There is no contracting out of our human solidarity. Few people can have passed through life without a desire at some time to recall words which have caused harm which he did not intend, or which he allowed himself half to intend.

The modern inventions of radio, television, the cinema and the microphone, have created means of mass persuasion whose irresponsible use, whose use for sectional ends, and for ends other than those of human good, constitute one of the major problems of our time. Broadcasting plays its part in the cold war. Nations employ monitoring services to discover what is being broadcast in other nations; but there is no monitoring in the service of truth, nor could there be. It was the spell-binding of Adolf Hitler, his skilful if passionate manipulation of vast audiences, which gave him the willing soldiers of the Third Reich. Nationalisms all over the world, to say nothing of Communism, are at it still. 'And who is my neighbour?' the scribe asked Jesus. One answer for to-day is that one's neighbour is not just some individual person: it may be a whole country. False witness against neighbouring countries is rarely condemned. Organised propaganda can bludgeon spiritual resistance to senselessness: it can also subtly change standards of judgment, so that a person does not realise that he has been caught in a trap of deception. In this field in particular our Lord's command to watch as well as pray should be a directive for twentieth-century Christians.

Very often what does most harm is the half-lie; truth manipulated can be falsehood's strongest weapon. The classic example of this is the Ems Telegram, of July 13, 1870, which precipitated the Franco-Prussian War. The King of Prussia sent a dispatch to his minister, Count Bis-

marck, indicating the nature of his negotiations with the representatives of France. When it had been sufficiently blue-
pencilled for publication its effect was completely changed.
Moltke exclaimed, 'The original was an order to retreat,
now it is a summons to charge.' This was done, of course,
with the press in view; and in 1905 Professor Holland Rose
could write: 'The story of the Franco-German dispute is
one of national jealousy carefully fanned for four years by
newspaper editors and popular speakers until a spark
sufficed to set Western Europe in a blaze.' He continued
prophetically: 'It is well that one of the chief dangers to the
peace of the modern world should be clearly recognized.
The centralization of governments and of population may
have its advantages; but over against them one must set
grave drawbacks; among those of a political kind the worst
are the growth of nervousness and excitability, and the
craving for sensation – qualities which undoubtedly tend to
embitter national jealousies at all times, and in the last case
to drive weak dynasties or Cabinets on to war. Certainly
Bismark's clever shifts to bring about a rupture in 1870
would have failed had not the atmosphere both of Paris and
Berlin been charged with electricity.'[1]

About twenty years later the late Julien Benda took up the
theme in his famous book, now too little read, *La Trahison
des Clercs*: 'The reader will already have perceived an all-
important factor in the impulses I have been describing.
Political passions rendered universal, coherent, homo-
geneous, permanent, preponderant – everyone can recognise
there to a great extent the work of the cheap daily political
newspaper. One cannot help reflecting and wondering
whether it may not be that inter-human wars are only just
beginning, when one thinks of this instrument for developing

---

[1] *The Development of the European Nations* (London, 1905), p. 49.
The two versions of the Ems Telegram are set out in C. Grant Robertson
Bismarck (London, 1918), pp. 496, 497. See also p. 270, n.

their own passions which men have just invented, or at east brought to a degree of power never seen before, to which they abandon themselves with all the expansion of their hearts every morning as soon as they awake.'[1] The populations to-day do not take the newspapers as seriously as that; but their power may be no less great because its effect is more on the unconscious than on the conscious mind. Benda was also writing prophetically; writing before the development of modern broadcasting; writing before the advent of Hitler; writing before the cold war, in which governments 'jam' the output of the radio stations of rival powers. 'Our age', said Benda, 'is indeed the age of the *intellectual organization of political hatreds*.'[2] We have seen that description verified up to the hilt.

An illustration, comparable almost to that of the Ems Telegram is provided in the autobiography of Viscount Templewood. As Sir Samuel Hoare he was Secretary of State for India. It was a great triumph when Mahatma Gandhi, the great leader of the campaign of passive resistance against the British in India agreed to come to London for the Round Table Conference on the future of the sub-continent. It was a greater triumph still when good relations were secured with him and genuine understanding. But all was nearly wasted by a piece of irresponsible and mendacious journalism. On his return he spent a few hours in Rome, where a reporter of the *Giornale d'Italia* concocted a fictitious interview in which he declared that 'he was returning to India to re-start at once his campaign against England, and that the Conference in London had served only to unmask the true intentions of England.' The Secretary of State was amazed; 'The threat attributed to him was so unlike his parting words to me in London that I at once telegraphed for its confirmation. The answer came from Gandhi himself, to the effect that he had made no such statement, and that the

[2] *Ibid.*, p. 21.

reported interview was a fake. Whilst this disclaimer brought me great relief, the harm was unfortunately done. The lie, like calumny in Don Basilio's famous song in *The Barber of Seville*, had already spread over the world, and had been accepted in London and Delhi as clear proof of Gandi's irreconcilable opposition. "We always told you so," said the diehard critics. "We always knew that he was our bitterest enemy." [1]

In Britain the rise of broadcasting, through its careful control by an independent monopoly, has been a check upon the extravagances of the popular press, so that a journalist can write: 'When the full history of the techniques of communication in the twentieth century is written, it may be judged that the popular newspaper proprietors were right in feeling acute alarm when the British Broadcasting Corporation first came into existence and began to broadcast news and comment. They were wrong in supposing that its rivalry would cause people to stop buying newspapers. It was more subtly and fundamentally dangerous than that: by seeking steadily to maintain certain standards of impartiality and objectivity, it has gradually, over the years, helped to teach people to stop *believing* newspapers, at any rate, of the more garish sort. This, in the long run, can only be in the interests of decent journalism as well as of the public.' [2]

There is such a thing as false witness against the dead; and this was a pastime, much applauded, among certain writers earlier in this century. The principle *De mortuis nil nisi bonum* is not, of course, admissible in historical research. The facts must be allowed to tell. But from believing the best of the departed the pendulum seemed to swing, in the 'twenties in Great Britain, to believing the worst. There were to be no more heroes. When a writer has happened on a piece of historical gossip which exactly fits his purpose of

[1] Viscount Templewood, *Nine Troubled Years* (London, 1954), p. 65.
[2] Tom Driberg, *Beaverbrook* (London, 1956), p. 215.

biographical denigration he does not always proceed to verify his references; as Lord Elton has shown that Lytton Strachey failed to do in his critical study of General Gordon in *Eminent Victorians*.[1]

In a law-court a witness swears that he will not only tell the truth, but the whole truth. That is an impossibility in daily newspapers, which are inevitably put together at great pace, and in which one man's reporting is subjected to cutting by another, and to another's provision of headlines, designed, perhaps, not so much to indicate the nature of the paragraphs which follow as to attract the eye and titillate the senses. Nevertheless steps need to be taken to allay that fear of the popular press which is so widely felt by public men to-day, many of whom have suffered by those who have so reported what they have said that it came to be almost the opposite of what they meant. In particular there is needed a commonly accepted code of the telephoned interview: if the man in the newspaper office were to read back over the telephone the sentences he intended to submit for publication, many shocks might be avoided. In Britain the Press Council can help here; but not, as yet, very much. It is unfortunate when men have to resort to the processes of law for the clearing of their characters: but this is sometimes both necessary and effective. The words of a great newspaper editor of a former generation are often quoted, and rightly so. In speaking of the conduct of a newspaper, C. P. Scott once declared: 'Fundamentally it implies honesty, cleanness, courage, fairness, a sense of duty to the reader and the community. The newspaper is of necessity something of a monopoly, and its first duty is to shun the temptations of a monopoly. Its primary task is the gathering of News. At the peril of its soul it must see that the supply is not tainted. Neither in what it gives nor in what it does not give, nor in the mode of presentation, must the unclouded face of Truth suffer

[1] See *General Gordon* (London, 1954), Book V, Anatomy of a Slander.

wrong. Comment is free, but facts are sacred. Propaganda, so called, by this means is hateful. The voice of opponents, no less than that of friends, has a right to be heard. Comment is also justly subject to a self-imposed restraint. It is well to be frank: it is even better to be fair.'[1]

It is not so easy as it sounds, especially in those many newspapers of our day which have adopted Lord North-cliffe's maxim of seeking the human angle to every story. Comment and reporting are often interwoven, and the method of presentation is everything. Yet happy is the country whose journalists endeavour to follow the example of a C. P. Scott. Frankness and fairness are a wholesome salt in social life, affecting realms far wider than those of journalism. It is interesting also to note that in the setting of a high standard the great editor of the *Manchester Guardian* did not avoid using language which verged on the theo-logical. '*At the peril of its soul* it must see that the supply is not tainted.' There are, alas, so-called newspapers to-day which hardly possess souls to be imperilled.

The command *Thou shalt not bear false witness against thy neighbour* is one broken as frequently as any other, and probably with the least sense of shame; yet in doing so, deep wounds can be caused. There are some lies which cannot be rebutted; but only lived down, in humble dependence upon the grace of God. In the early days of the Salvation Army the attacks upon its soldiers by mob violence and the mis-representation of its motives in the public press must have been hard to bear: but General Booth's son recalled: 'When I have gone to him, perhaps, with some infamous newspaper attack, and in my indignation have said, "This is really more than we can stand", he has replied, "Bramwell, fifty years hence it will matter very little indeed how these people treated us: it will matter a great deal how we dealt with the

---

[1] *Manchester Guardian*, May 6th, 1926. Quoted J. L. Hammond, *C. P. Scott* (London, 1934), p. 95, n.

work of God." [1] And a Christian does well to recall that his Master fulfilled the prophecy of the suffering servant of the Lord, who was 'brought as a lamb to the slaughter, and as a sheep that before her shearers is dumb, so he openeth not his mouth.' [2] It is recorded of Christ that 'when he reviled he reviled not again.' [3] It is right that the attacks of falsehood should be answered; that calumnies against the Church should be exposed: but it were better to go unprotected than to give a lie for a lie. That is the temptation of all who enter upon controversy, however high may be their motives.

Every local church, moreover, must face the temptation which confronts every form of society, that of being a group of gossiping people, whose gossip passes imperceptibly into slander. The sanctimonious spreader of half-truths can be as dangerous as the person engaged in the same pastime who makes no pretence of religion; more dangerous, indeed, for Christians have to remember that their Master has placed His reputation in their hands. The evil done by gossip and whispering, by what have come to be called smear-campaigns has often been analysed and held to ridicule: perhaps never more effectively than by the anonymous seventeenth-century author of *The Whole Duty of Man*.

'Of false reports there may be two sorts: the one when a man says something of his neighbour, which he directly knows to be false; the other, when possibly he has some slight surmise or jealousie of the thing, but that upon such weak grounds that it is as likely to be false as true. In either of these cases there is a great guilt lies upon the reporter. That there doth so in the first of them nobody will doubt, every one acknowledging that it is the greatest baseness to invent a lie of another; but there is as little reason to question the other, for he that reports a thing as a truth, which is but un-

[1] Quoted, St. John Ervine, *God's Soldier* (London, 1934), vol. i, p. 446.
[2] Isaiah 53. 7.
[3] 1. Peter 2. 23.

certain, is a liar also: or if he do not report it as a certainty, but only as a probability, yet then, though he be not guilty of the lie, yet he is of the injustice of robbing his neighbour of his credit; for there is such an aptness in men to believe ill of others, that any the lightest jealousy will, if once it be spread abroad, serve for that purpose; and sure it is a most horrible injustice upon every slight surmise and fancy to hazard the bringing so great an evil upon another, especially when it is considered, that those surmises commonly spring rather from some sensoriousness, peevishness, or malice in the surmiser, than from any real fault in the person so suspected.'

Of the Whisperer he writes that this is 'he that goes about from one to another and privately vents his slanders, not out of an intent by that means to make them less public, but rather more; this trick of delivering them by way of secret, being the way to make them both more believed, and more spoken of too; for he that receives such a tale as a secret from one, thinks to please somebody else, by delivering it as a secret to him also; and so it passes from one hand to another, till at last it spread over a whole town. This sort of slanderer is of all others the most dangerous, for he works in the dark, ties all he speaks to, not to own him as the author; so that whereas in the more public accusations, the party may have some means of clearing himself and detecting his accuser, like a secret poison, works incurable effects, before ever the man discern it.'[1]

The condemnation of the tale-bearer is found in all traditional wisdom, not least in that of the Jews.

'He that goeth about as a talebearer revealeth secrets:
But he that is of a faithful spirit concealeth the matter.'[2]

This is fairly obvious. A more searching analysis is found:

[1] Edition edited W. B. Hawkins (London, 1842), pp. 208–211.
[2] Prov. 11. 13.

F

'The words of a whisperer are as dainty morsels,
And they go down to the innermost parts of the belly.'[1]

Again we read that a whisperer alienateth his friends;[2] and
the sage advice, 'Meddle not with him that openeth wide his
lips.'[3]

And again:

'For lack of wood the fire goeth out:
And where there is no whisperer contention ceaseth.'[4]

In the New Testament also there is condemnation of 'strife,
jealousy, wraths, factions, backbiting, whisperings, swellings,
tumults.'[5] St. Paul spoke from experience of all of these; and
he had instigated some of them in his time. His arraignment
in Romans of the vices of the Gentiles – in which he seems
to range over most of the commandments – has the sin of
malicious speech at its heart:

'Being filled with all unrighteousness, wickedness,
covetousness, maliciousness; full of envy, murder, strife,
deceit, malignity; whisperers, backbiters, hateful to God,
insolent, haughty, boastful, inventors of evil things, disobedient to parents, without understanding, covenant-
breakers, without natural affection, unmerciful.'[6]

The basic idea behind it all is set out in Leviticus 19. 16,
'Thou shalt not go up and down as a talebearer among thy
people . . . I am the Lord.' In a world belonging to the God
of truth, untruth is rebellion against Him.

Falsehood is more closely woven into our social fabric
than is commonly realised; and where it is realised it produces, not an endeavour to extirpate it, but an attitude of
cynicism, a general assumption that all men are liars, some
of them more consciously so than others, some of them more

---

[1] Prov. 18. 8.   [2] Prov. 16. 28.   [3] Prov. 20. 19.
[4] Prov. 16. 20.   [5] 2. Cor. 12. 20.   [6] Rom. 1. 29–31.

successfully so. Thus the currency of human conduct becomes debased; confidence is undermined and loyalties become changeable and chancy. If there be no God of truth,
adherence to truth has lost much of its sanction. Why *not*
commit perjury if one's first act in a law-court is to swear by
an almighty God in whom one does not believe? So lies
increase. There are convenient lies, and sentimental lies,
and contemptuous lies. The two latter are often employed in
speaking to people weaker than oneself; to a child, to an old
person, to a member of another race. A lie to any one of
these is a failure to treat him as a person, to treat him with
respect; and, as such, it is deeply resented. A child's questions about sex, for example, are not to be answered by
giving a lecture on biology – which would be far from being
the whole truth in the matter. But on this, as on most other
subjects, a child quickly realises that he is being told an untruth; or that evasion of his question is masquerading as an
answer to it. He does not need a complete answer; he needs
one in terms of his understanding and experience. The
normal child accepts this; and is not afraid to ask again. The
question of telling the truth to those whose expectation of
life is short, and those who are actually dying, is one from
which doctors and relatives turn aside, for fear of causing
pain, or for lack of personal courage. There are, of course,
cases where it is wiser that the truth should be withheld.
But they are not so numerous as is usually supposed.

Because truth in human relationships is so difficult –
because it is so difficult to be fair to those whose opinions
are different from our own – it is valuable that the prayers
of the Church are so often prayers for those very things
which are not to be achieved by human striving, but only
through the indwelling of the Spirit of Truth Himself. This
prayer is uttered again and again in the Psalms, as the ideal is
also stated:

Make me a clean heart, O God: and renew a right spirit within me.[1]

My help cometh of God: who preserveth them that are true of heart.[2]

Lord, who shall dwell in thy tabernacle: or who shall rest upon thy holy hill?

Even he that leadeth an uncorrupt life: and doeth the thing which is right, and speaketh the truth from his heart.

He that hath used no deceit in his tongue, nor done evil to his neighbour: and hath not slandered his neighbour.[3]

Let the words of my mouth, and the meditation of my heart: be always acceptable in thy sight.

O Lord: my strength, and my redeemer.[4]

I said, I will take heed to my ways: that I offend not in my tongue.

I will keep my mouth as it were with a bridle: while the ungodly is in my sight.[5]

It is well for us to ask for God's help. We need it greatly. To tell the truth and to discern the truth is rarely so easy as many imagine. There are complicated situations in which the truth seems ever to be in retreat or in hiding. If falsehood is to be cast out of life there is need for much more of that fundamental re-thinking which Jesus called repentance. Truth in human dealings depends upon respect for human people: it is dependent upon the fact that the person whom one is tempted to slander is one's neighbour. The instructions to a Christian about his neighbour are direct and simple. It is to love him as oneself. Who is sufficient for these things? No one, in his own power. But even in the complicated world of to-day God's Spirit is the Spirit of truth. At the heart of

[1] Psalm 51. 10.   [2] Psalm 8 11.   [3] Psalm 15. 1–3.
[4] Psalm 19, 14, 15.   [5] Psalm 39. 1, 2.

the universe – such is the Christian faith – is no lying mockery; no malicious trifler; but One who is Himself the source of truth; who has treated us as real people by showing us the truth in Jesus; by being prepared always to enable us to grasp more of His truth. But if we break the covenant with others we break it with Him, A just God demands justice in the dealings of those who profess to serve Him. Who is sufficient for these things? The Commandment *Thou shalt not bear false witness against thy neighbour* points directly to the pattern prayer of Jesus: 'Forgive us our trespasses as we forgive them that trespass against us.'

X

THE DISEASE OF COVETOUSNESS

Thou shalt not covet thy neighbour's house, thou shalt not covet thy neighbour's wife, nor his manservant, nor his maidservant, nor his ox, nor his ass, nor anything that is thy neighbour's. *Exodus 20. 17.*

Woe to them that devise iniquity and work evil upon their beds! when the morning is light, they practise it, because it is in the power of their hand. And they covet fields and seize them; and houses, and take them away: and they oppress a man and his house, even a man and his heritage. *Micah 2. 1, 2.*

Ye cannot serve God and mammon. *Matthew 6. 24.*

And Jesus looking upon him loved him, and said unto him, One thing thou lackest: go, sell whatsoever thou hast, and give to the poor, and thou shalt have treasure in heaven: and come, follow me. But his countenance fell at that saying, and he went away sorrowful: for he was one that had great possessions.

Mark 10. 21, 22.

Covetousness, which is idolatry. *Colossians 3. 5.*

I had not known sin, except through the law: for I had not known coveting, except the law had said, Thou shalt not covet: but sin, finding occasion, wrought in me through the commandment all manner of coveting . . . And the commandment, which was unto life, this I found to be unto death: for sin, finding occasion, through the commandment beguiled me, and through it slew me . . . O wretched man that I am! who shall deliver me out of the body of this death? I thank God through Jesus Christ our Lord. *Romans 7. 7–11, 24, 25.*

For ye know the grace of our Lord Jesus Christ, that, though he was rich, yet for your sakes he became poor, that ye through his poverty might become rich. *2. Corinthians 8. 9.*

As having nothing, and yet possessing all things.

2. Corinthians 6. 10.

O God, the protector of all that trust in thee, without whom nothing is strong, nothing is holy; increase and multiply upon us thy mercy; that, thou being our ruler and guide, we may so pass through things temporal, that we finally lose not the things eternal: Grant this, O heavenly Father, for Jesus Christ's sake our Lord. Amen. *Collect for the Fourth Sunday after Trinity.*

———

A SPEAKER before the American Society of Medical Jurisprudence was sketching the 'chain reaction' which culminates in the act of murder:

'An adolescent likes to have a girl; in order to have a proper standing with her, he has to have a car. He steals one. To entertain her, he needs money. He sees all around him false prototypes of what a real girl wants.

'He learns about guns. He shoots.'[1]

The term 'chain reaction' is a new one; but the fact is as old as humanity. There was an Israelite king who wanted to live up to the expectations of the princess from the more powerful neighbouring kingdom whom he had married. To have proper standing with Jezebel, Ahab felt that he must round out his possessions by getting hold of Naboth's vineyard. The story changes there, because it was the Queen, who came from a circle which was unaccustomed to religion placing restraints upon the action of men in power, who

[1] Quoted, George Godwin, *Crime and Social Action* (London 1956), p. 61.

planned the murder, while it was the King who felt the remorse.[1] Behind both these typical happenings, in the twentieth century A.D. and in the ninth century B.C., there lies covetousness. The man who is content does not turn to crime. There is, indeed, what has been called a divine discontent, a burning passion for righteousness, a refusal to accept injustice done to the weak, which has sometimes driven men to action which has crossed the bounds of legality. There are some men with whom one would have been proud to have been in prison. This is very different from the nagging desire for increased and better possessions, for a position of greater honour, a desire for what another has and you have not, which is a poison in social relationships; a poison more harmful to the envious than to the envied. Yet it is the motive of covetousness that business excites to sell its wares and politics invokes to secure its votes. There are times when it appears to be the principal driving force in society.

Thou shalt not covet thy neighbour's house, thou shalt not covet thy neighbour's wife, nor his servant, nor his maid, nor his ox, nor his ass, nor anything that is his. It may seem strange that house is mentioned before wife; but the word suggests not a building so much as the whole complex of human relationships which makes a household, of which a man's wife is both integrator and ornament. In Deuteronomy, however, the wife comes first.[2] Rabbi Goldman points out that 'according to both decalogues, the wife belongs to the husband in a sense in which the husband does not belong to the wife. At any rate, neither reads: "You shall not covet your neighbour's husband."'[3] In societies in which there is a closer approximation to sexual equality this converse needs to be remembered. Covetousness of all kinds seems to be dealt with in this command: the adulterous desire for another's partner; the desire for another's position; the desire for

---

[1] 2. Kings 21.   [2] Deut. 5. 21.   [3] *Op. cit.*, p. 189.

another's possessions. When St. Paul wrote to the Romans he could cite it in the simple form, 'Thou shalt not covet.'[1] The Authorised Version makes him use the word 'covet' also in a good sense, in 'Covet earnestly the best gifts'[2] and 'covet to prophesy.'[3] But the verb is different in the Greek; later versions translate it 'desire earnestly.' Yet it is human experience how easily the earnest desire to serve becomes confused with the coveting of a position. Mixed motives are commoner than any others; and most commonly there is covetousness in the mixture.

The other commandments, with the partial exception of the first, are all concerned with outward acts; with deeds which can be isolated and punished; and we have seen that for the breaking of seven of them death was the enacted penalty. But the last commandment is different. It steps into the territory of the New Testament; for it is concerned with motive. Covetousness in itself is not a crime which can be punished; though there may spring from it all the crimes in the calendar. Micah has a description of the chain reaction:

> 'Woe to them that devise iniquity and work evil upon their beds! when the morning is light they practise it, because it is in the power of their hand. And they covet fields, and seize them; and houses and take them away: and they oppress a man and his house, even a man and his heritage.'[4]

The teaching of Jesus was that evil came from within. 'There is nothing from without the man, that going into him can defile him: but the things that proceed out of the man are those that defile a man.'[5] This was contrary to much Jewish opinion in His own day; and to much Christian opinion in our own. 'So far as the Decalogue was concerned,' writes Canon Lindsay Dewar, 'there was only one of the Ten Com-

[1] Rom. 13. 9. [2] 1. Cor. 12. 31. [3] 1. Cor. 14. 39.
[4] Micah 2. 1, 2. [5] Mark 7. 15.

mandments which adopted this standpoint – the last, in which explicit reference is made to the internal disposition of the mind: "Thou shalt not covet." What our Lord does is to reinterpret the whole of the Decalogue in the light of this.'[1]

Our Lord's insistence upon inward motive often led Him to outward action; and the first thing He did when He came to Jerusalem – with all the exciting events of the triumphal entry behind Him, with all the popular support it presaged – was to attack covetousness. 'Who is this?' the people of Jerusalem had asked; and His fellow-pilgrims from the North had answered proudly, 'This is Jesus, the prophet of Nazareth of Galilee.'[2] And now He was acting in a prophetic way. He entered the Court of the Gentiles: the one place where the outsider should have a footing within the Temple precincts; the place above all where non-Jews should be treated with respect – and found that they had been crowded out by a haggling bunch of traders; and by representatives of the high priest's family, which did very well out of the money-changing. 'Is it not written, My house shall be called a house of prayer for all the nations? but ye have made it a den of robbers.'[3] So scathing were His words, so imperious was His presence, so decisive was His action, that they knew they had to go. In the Ober-Ammergau Passion Play it is a chorus of outraged traders which later cries, 'Crucify him!' Few things provoke men to bitterness so quickly as those which touch their pockets. The early Church also was to discover this. At Philippi it was men who felt cheated of their gains, through the exorcism of a mediumistic girl who was their creature, who 'saw that the hope of their gains was gone'[4], who instigated the uproar that placed Paul and Silas, bleeding – but singing hymns, none the less – in the stocks. At Ephesus it was idol-makers who were afraid of losing their trade. 'This Paul hath persuaded and turned away much people, saying that they be no gods, which are

[1] *Op. cit.*, p. 25.   [2] Matt. 21. 11.   [3] Mark 11. 17.   [4] Acts 16. 19.

made with hands: and not only is there danger that this our trade come into disrepute; but also that the temple of the great goddess Diana be made of no account, and that she should be deposed from her magnificence, whom all Asia and the world worshippeth. And when they heard this, they were filled with wrath, and cried out, saying, Great is Diana of the Ephesians. And the city was filled with confusion.'[1] Self-interest came first; though it was useful that it could be supported by a patriotic cry. It was neither the first nor the last time in history that patriotic emotions have been engendered by the interests of a small group of men.

In what has rightly been called an acquisitive society, envy and covetousness are a mainspring of acquisitiveness: they loosen the flood-gates which allow the channels of currency to flow. Examples can easily be found in popular advertising. The Christmas display in the shops of Oxford Street has been called a mile-long incitement to covetousness. *She's lucky – She's even got . . . Shoes* expresses it directly; but envy is more often merely hinted at, the spirit more subtly evoked. An American writer once commented: 'The community that can be trained to desire change, to want new things even before the old have been entirely consumed, yields a market to be measured more by desires than needs. And man's desires can be developed so that they will greatly overshadow his needs. . . . Human nature very conveniently presents a variety of strings upon which an appreciative sales manager can play fortissimo . . . Threats, fear, beauty, sparkle, persuasion and careful as well as wild-cat exaggeration were thrown at the American buying public as a continuous and terrifying barrage. . . . And so desire was enthroned in the minds of the American consumer, and was served abjectly by the industries that had enthroned it.'[2]

[1] Acts 19. 26–28.

[2] Paul Mazur, quoted Denys Thompson, *Voice of Civilisation*, An Enquiry into Advertising (London, 1943), p. 71.

Sales-resistance is certainly a necessary part of any liberal education. Weakness here is one of the commonest forms of personal indiscipline. Even people who are not naturally covetous may, unless they are careful, be made covetous by the pressures of society.

At the end of the nineteenth century Thorstein Veblen examined our pecuniary society in his famous book *The Theory of The Leisure Class*. Its very chapter headings remain a recognisable indictment: Pecuniary Emulation; Conspicuous Leisure; The Pecuniary Standard of Living; Pecuniary Canons of Taste; Dress as an Expression of the Pecuniary Culture; The Higher Learning as the Expression of the Pecuniary Culture. He satirised a wealthy class which lived its life in public, before spectators, as consciously and as constantly as any Roman emperor. That was in America. There were hardly less edifying parallels in England. 'The *rentier* and his ways,' wrote Mr. R. H. Tawney in 1921, 'how familiar they were in England before the war! A public school and then club life in Oxford and Cambridge, and then another club in town; London in June, when London is pleasant, the moors in August, and pheasants in October, Cannes in December and hunting in February and March; and a whole world of rising bourgeoisie eager to imitate them, sedulous to make their expensive watches keep time with this preposterous calendar.'[1] Since then the British exemplars of this way of life have been impoverished; and the leisured classes in the United States have learned to laugh at themselves. But social emulation remains.

The late Arthur Clutton-Brock pointed out that Veblen's theory was ingenious but imperfect, since it is not only the rich, but all men, rich and poor alike, who indulge in conspicuous waste. Our whole community is engaged in it. He found the aptest picture of our society in Blake's figure of a child which stretches out its hand and cries – *I want – I*

[1] *The Acquisitive Society* (London, 1921), p. 37.

want. 'Without knowing what our wants are, we spend more and more money in satisfying them; and always the process becomes more and more expensive, being indeed valued because of its expense.'[1] The social revolution in Great Britain has brought about a much more equitable distribution of resources; but it has created a population crying out 'I want', people whose appetite for possession has been stimulated by what they already have. It reaches a fantastic point when it is seriously suggested that old age pensioners should receive more, not primarily for their own needs, but for the good of the community. For if they had more money they would be able to buy television sets and other 'consumer goods' – and this would keep the wheels of industry turning. The warning cry of to-day is 'Your standard of living is in danger.' But we seldom ask what our standard of living really is. The value of productivity, at least for the home market, is one of the less explored assumptions of our time.

For what do we want? Certainly more houses. Certainly less drudgery. But do we really need more motor-cars? The accident figures at least sound a warning note; and it is significant that when petrol rationing had to be introduced in Great Britain in 1956 owing to the Suez crisis, the death-roll immediately declined. Mr. Lewis Mumford's discussion of these things in terms of New York has significance for those who live in or near any modern centre of population. 'Were the eruption of vehicles and buildings in and around New York a natural phenomenon, like Vesuvius, there would be little use discussing it; lava inexorably carves its own channels through the landscape. But the things that spoil life in New York and its environs were all made by men, and can be changed by men as soon as they are willing to change their minds. Most of our contributions to planned chaos are caused by private greed and public miscalculation rather than

[1] *The Necessity of Art* (London, 1924), p. 19.

irrational wilfulness.'[1] The displacement of private greed
demands more than a change of mind; though that is one
part of the process of repentance which every reformer in
history has sought to initiate.

Meanwhile we are faced by the terrifying prospects of the
atomic age. The morning's newspaper at the time of writing.[2]
records a demonstration non-stop flight of three American
jet bombers round the world in forty-five hours, by planes
designed to carry hydrogen bombs, and which carried out a
mock nuclear bomb raid on the way. The commander of the
United States Strategic Air Command described the flight as
'a demonstration of the Command's capabilities to strike any
target on the face of the earth.' This makes us think about
Deep Shelters in the Nuclear Age. But what of *Covetousness in
the Nuclear Age!* Here is a prospect which also has its terrors.
In Great Britain the major emphasis so far is on the use of
atomic power for peaceful purposes; and in this enterprise
Britain is at present in the lead. But how is this power to be
used? Just to make more and more things? A paradise of
consumer goods in a covetous world does not sound very like
a paradise at all.

During the last war Dr. Marjorie Reeves, concerned about
the influences which were being brought to bear upon young
people, analysed the prevailing values and attitudes which
were being taught them through the pervasive influences of
poster, film, newspaper, and the conversation of many of
their elders. She reduced the headings to four, and showed
that they were in diametrical opposition to the Christian
understanding of life and its purposes. The language is now
slightly 'dated', as are the objects of acquisitive desire, but
the indictment remains:

'1. The happiest person is he who possesses most
     material possession: the chief satisfaction in life is to

[1] In *The New Yorker*, April 2, 1955.
[2] January 19, 1957.

get and get more and more. If you've got a bicycle, you must get a car, then perhaps another, then a radio, then a gramophone.

'2. The law of the world is competition: the only sensible way to act is to get on, to climb up, to push some one else down.

'3. Work is a nuisance to be avoided by every device possible; the less work you do the more lucky you are: the further up the tree you climb the less work you do, whilst the "big toff" at the top of the tree does not work a all.

'4. The powers that rule this world – known as "they" – are untrustworthy and arbitrary, to be tricked and out-witted as often as possible and obeyed as seldom as possible.'

The Christian antitheses to these propositions were shorter. They ran as follows:

'1. It is more blessed to give than to receive.

'2. We are members one of another.

'3. He that is greatest among you let him be the servant of all.

'4. God rules this world and God is love.'

Envy can be of position as much as of possession – as the above catalogue reveals. This is a sinfulness of which men in the organised life of the Church need particularly to be aware. It is always hard to realise that the most responsible positions can only be for the few; and it is well also to remember that there are faults in your own life, glaringly obvious, perhaps, to others, of which you are the last to become aware. There is no sin more corrosive than pride; nor is there any to which those who make a profession of religion are more prone. 'Bended kness, while you are clothed with pride; heavenly petitions, while you are hoarding up treasures upon earth; holy devotions, while you live in the follies of the world; prayers of meekness and charity, while your heart is the seat of spite and resentment; hours of prayer, while you give up days and years to idle diversions, impertinent visits, and foolish pleasures; are as absurd, unacceptable services to God, as forms of thanksgiving from a person that lives in repinings and discontent.'[1] Cranmer was right to insert the Ten Commandments within the setting of the *Kyrie*, so that after the recitation of each there is the response from the congregation – and surely from the heart of the minister. *Lord, have mercy upon us.*

The words just quoted from William Law bring us very near to the need of Saul of Tarsus before his conversion. The Tenth Commandment played an important part in his spiritual development; preparing him for the revolutionary change by which he rejected Pharisaism. He came to realise that though he kept all the external commandments, there was an internal commandment he had not kept, nay, could not keep, without help from outside. 'It was', writes Dr. Vidler, 'the devastating discovery of his inner guilt that convinced him that there was no hope for him or for his nation or for the world, unless he was delivered from bondage to the law, and unless there was imparted to him a kind of inward righteousness which he could never achieve by himself. It was the sting in the tail of the decalogue that convicted him of sin, and brought him to the place where he put his whole trust in Jesus Christ as the universal Lord and Saviour.'[2]

It was Paul's experience that striving could not make him

[1] William Law, *A Serious Call to a Devout and Holy Life*, ch. 9.

[2] *Christian Belief and the World* (London, 1956), p. 104.

good. Something was lacking. He was facing an enemy whose measure he had only begun to take. 'For the good which I would I do not: but the evil which I would not, that I practise.'[1] He knew he should not envy; but went on doing it: indeed, the very fact of its being forbidden made it all the more attractive to that inner self which he was unable to master. This is how William Sanday and A. C. Headlam, in their great commentary on Romans, paraphrased this part of the apostle's involved but deeply felt argument: 'I knew the sinfulness of covetous or illicit desire only by the Law saying, "Thou shalt not covet." But the lurking Sin within me started into activity, and by the help of that express command, provoking to that which it prohibited, led me into all kinds of conscious and sinful covetousness. For without Law to bring it out Sin lies dead – inert and passive. And while sin was dead, I – my inner self – was alive, in happy unconsciousness, following my bent with no pangs of conscience excited by Law. But then came this Tenth Commandment; and with its coming Sin awoke to life, while I – sad and tragic contrast – died the living death of sin, precursor of eternal death. And the commandment which was given to point men the way to life, this very commandment was found in my case to lead to death. For Sin took advantage of it, and by the help of the commandment – at once confronting me with the knowledge of right and provoking me to do that which was wrong – it betrayed me, so that I fell; and the commandment was the weapon with which it slew me.'[2]

That was not the end of the story, as every Christian reader knows. While distraught by an intolerable inner tension, Paul's eyes were blinded by a light from without. He

---

[1] Rom. 7. 19.

[2] *A Critical and Exegetical Commentary on the Epistle to the Romans* (International Critical Commentary. 5th edit. Edinburgh, 1902), p. 177, paraphrase of Rom. 7. 6–11.

fell to the ground as one dead. But when he was able to go forward again he knew that the tension was over. Golgotha had achieved what Sinai could never achieve. 'O wretched man that I am! who shall deliver me out of the body of this death? I thank my God through Jesus Christ our Lord.'[1]

For the cure of covetousness it is to the New Testament we must look. Jesus pointed to the source of trouble in the inner life. Man is a creature that needs to be mastered. If he be mastered by another man the end is degradation: if he be mastered merely by an ideal the end is frustration. A Christian believes that he only finds the fulness of life, release from the mean grasping to which his nature tends, when he has responded to the love of God, revealed in Christ whom he has accepted as Lord. St. James, at a far lower pitch of intensity, indicated the same tension as St. Paul. 'Whence come wars and whence come fightings among you? Ye list, and have not; ye kill and covet, and cannot obtain.'[2] For him the cure came through the sense of proportion which prayer brings: 'Humble yourselves in the sight of the Lord, and he shall exalt you.'[3] It may be pointed out that this sense of proportion does not demand the Christian revelation; and St. James himself quotes the Old Testament saying, 'God resisteth the proud but giveth grace to the humble.'[4] But how can a man become humble?

Bishop Edward King of Lincoln used to say that humility does not consist in making yourself humble, but in having a right relationship to great things. The cure for covetousness does not consist in caring less; but in caring more for what really matters; caring more for people because you see in them the image of God, because they are brothers for whom Christ died. 'Set your affection upon things above,'[5] as the familiar Easter Gospel has it: and again, St. Paul's prayer for his Philippian friends was 'that ye may approve the

[1] Rom. 7. 24.   [2] James 4. 1 ff.   [3] James 4. 11.
[4] Prov. 3. 34, Psalm 31 8. 6.   [5] Col. 3. 2.

things that are excellent.'[1] Buddhism sees the way of salvation through the elimination of desire; Christianity through
its mastery and direction. 'Desire earnestly the best gifts,'
wrote St. Paul, and then went on to the greatest gift of all,
the indispensable gift of charity. The word *gift* is important.
He was speaking of a gift which comes from God.

Men have first to be humbled before they become humble,
not naturally humble, but supernaturally humble. St. Paul
again points the way, when he begins his great passage in
Philippians, 'Have this mind in you, which was also in
Christ Jesus.' Indeed this passage appears to make a conscious reply to the covetousness of our first parents. In the
myth of the Fall, Adam and Eve regarded equality with God
as something to be grasped at. They wanted, like the people
of to-day: they wanted to be as gods. And because they
reached so high, they fell. Jesus did the opposite, with
opposite results:

'Have this mind in you, which was also in Christ Jesus:
who, being in the form of God, counted it not a thing to be
grasped at to be on an equality with God, but emptied
himself, taking the form of a slave, being made in the likeness of men; and being found in fashion as a man, he
humbled himself, becoming obedient even unto death,
yea, the death of the cross. Wherefore also God highly
exalted him, and gave unto him the name which is above
every name; that in the name of Jesus every knee should
bow, of things in heaven, and things on earth, and things
under the earth, and that every tongue should confess that
Jesus Christ is Lord, to the glory of God the Father.'[2]

It is as men echo that heavenly worship – as they look to that
throne where is a Lamb slain from the foundation of the
earth – that they obtain guidance to see the significance of

[1] Phil. 1. 10   [2] Phil. 2. 5–11.

the old commandments given on Sinai and grace to fulfil them. St. Paul also wrote of 'covetousness which is idolatry.'[1] Idolatry is false worship; delight in the created at the expense of the Creator. To come through the created to the Creator is to approach that fear of the Lord which is the beginning of wisdom. It is worship that we need; worship which both humbles and exalts; worship which unites men in the selfless passion of adoration; worship which drives men out into the world to do God's will.

Who is sufficient for these things?

Lord, have mercy upon us, and write all these thy laws in our hearts, we beseech thee.

[1] Col. 3. 5.

INDEX OF SCRIPTURAL REFERENCES
IN THE TEXT AND NOTES

[The figures printed in *italics* refer to page numbers in the book]

OLD TESTAMENT AND APOCRYPHA

Genesis

9. 6	*96, 100*
11	*76*

Exodus

20. 2	*9, 19*
2, 3	*24*
3	*23*
4–6	*32, 34*
7	*53*
8–11	*66, 72*
12	*84*
13	*96*
14	*115*
15	*132*
16	*147*
17	*166*
21. 16	*132*
22. 10, 11	*57*
31. 13, 17	*73*
32. 1, 24	*36*

Leviticus

19. 12	*53, 57*
16	*147*
18, 33, 34	*75*

33	*78*
25. 23	*86*
26. 12	*19*

Numbers

31. 9	*35*

Deuteronomy

5. 12–15	*72*
15	*74, 79*
14, 15	*66*
16	*94*
21	*168*
6. 4–5	*11*
5–10	*20*
20–21	*9*
7. 7, 8	*74*
8. 7, 8	*125*
12. 11	*62*
16. 2	*62*
24. 19–22	*132, 138*
26. 2	*62*

Judges

3. 5, 6	*125*
17. 6	*134*
21. 25	*134*

Ruth
    1. 16, 17   *57*

1 Samuel
    20. 13   *57*
    25. 22   *57*
    26. 19   *24*

2 Samuel
    12. 1–7   *115*

1 Kings
    12. 28, 29   *36*
    22.   *99*

2 Kings
    2. 24   *49*
    5. 17   *24*
    18. 4   *35*
    19. 10   *51*
    21.   *168*

1 Chronicles
    29. 15   *86*

Psalms
    8. 11   *164*
    15. 1–3   *147, 164*
    19. 14, 15   *164*
    27. 12   *84*
    34. 8   *20*
    39. 1, 2   *164*
    12   *86*
    51. 6   *147*
    10   *164*
    68. 5, 6   *84*
    99. 3   *53*
    103. 13   *93*

    106. 6–8   *9*
    107. 4–8   *9*
    111. 9   *53*
    119. 54   *148*
    124. 1–3   *99*
    128. 1–4   *88*
    137. 1, 4   *37*
    138. 6   *178*
    148. 12   *84*

Proverbs
    3. 34   *178*
    11. 13   *161*
    16. 20, 28   *162*
    18. 8   *162*
    9   *132*
    20. 19   *162*
    25. 21, 22   *96, 114*

Isaiah
    1. 13, 14   *68*
    25. 7   *26*
    40. 28–31   *23*
    44. 6   *25*
    14–19   *38*
    45. 21–23   *25*
    53. 7   *160*
    55. 7   *63*
    57. 15   *63*

Jeremiah
    14. 9   *52*
    17. 5, 6   *48*

Ezekiel
    18. 30–32   *32*
    20. 12, 20   *73*

Hosea

2. 8, 9	27
14	126
4. 11	126
8. 5, 6	36
11. 1	9

Amos

2. 6	136
8	137
3. 1, 2	25
2	75
5. 7	75
11	137
9. 7	26

Micah

2. 1, 2	166

Wisdom of Solomon

11. 21, 22	23
14. 11	32

1 Maccabees

2. 32–38	69

NEW TESTAMENT

St. Matthew

1. 21	63
5. 21, 22	96
27, 28	115
28	128
29	128
33–37	59
43–45	96
6. 19–22	132, 139
22, 23	61, 150
24	166

10. 21, 22	166
12. 11, 12	74
39	127
16. 4	127
18. 20	53, 62
19. 4–6	116, 119
5	90
9	129
21. 11	170
28–31	147
31	128
22. 37	11
25. 45	109
26. 63	59
27. 38	133

St. Mark

2. 27	66
27, 28	69
3. 2, 5	74
3–5	109
6. 7–9	140
7. 9–11	88
21–22	128
22	150
8. 38	127
9. 45	110
10. 25	137
26	138
29, 30	84
11. 17	170
12. 30	11
40	137

St. Luke

2. 51–52	84
3. 8	75
6. 4	73

St. Luke

    6. 38   *132*
    8. 2   *128*
    10. 27   *11*
    12. 16–21   *137*
    19. 8   *137*

St. John

    4. 23, 24   *32*
    5. 17   *66*
    8. 8–11   *127*
    19. 26, 27   *85*
    20. 1   *67*

Acts of the Apostles

    14. 15, 16   *49*
    16. 19   *170*
    17. 16   *35*
    19. 26–28   *171*
    20. 7   *67*

Romans

    1. 25   *56*
    7. 6–11   *177*
       7–11, 24, 25 *166*
       19   *177*
       24   *54, 178*
    10. 11–13   *53*
    11. 12   *50*
       33–36   *23*
    12. 11   *145*
       20   *114*
    13. 9   *169*
       10   *96*
       12–14   *116*

1 Corinthians

    6. 19–20   *116, 124*
    8. 10, 11   *43*
    10. 25–29   *43*

    12. 31   *169*
    14. 39   *169*

2 Corinthians

    1. 20   *59*
    6. 10   *167*
    9. 10   *139*
    12. 20   *162*

Galatians

    1. 20   *59*
    3. 21   *14*
       28   *76*

Ephesians

    3. 5   *139*
       13, 14   *93*
    4. 15   *146*
       28   *139*
    5. 28   *133*
    6. 4   *89*
       1–14   *84*

Philippians

    1. 8   *59*
       10   *179*
    2. 5–11   *179*
       9–11   *63*
    3. 8   *89*
    4. 7, 8   *128*

Colossians

    1. 12–15   *33*
       13   *79*
       15   *49*
    3. 2   *178*
       5   *166, 180*
       11   *76*
       21   *89*

1 Thessalonians
    1. 9   *49*
    5. 24   *148*

Hebrews
    1. 1, 2   *18*
    10. 23   *147*
    11. 13   *10*

James
    1. 26   *147*
    3. 2–10   *153*
    4. 1, 11   *178*

1 Peter
    2. 21–24   *97*
    23   *160*

1 John
    1. 5   *23*
    3. 15   *114*
    5. 21   *33, 35*

Revelation
    1. 10   *67, 80*
    21. 3   *23*

INDEX OF NAMES

Abraham, 18, 21, 75

Africans, 76, 78, 106, 108, 118, 134 ff, 143

Ahab, 99

Aquinas, St. Thomas, 12

Arabia, 68

Arnold, Matthew, 16

Assyria, 67

Atherton, Gertrude, 118

Augustus, Emperor, 39, 43, 44

Babel, Tower of, 76

Babylon, 35, 37, 39, 67

Baillie, John, 16

Ballantyne, R. M., 134 ff

Balleine, G. R., 145 n

Barlow (Report), 91

Barrow, R. H., 44 n

Beaverbrook, Lord, 157 n

Benda, Julien, 155

Berdyaev, N., 101 n

Berggrav, Bishop Eivand, 105

Bertholet, Alfred, 39

Bethel, 36

Bettenson, H., 81 n

Beveridge, Lord, 98

Bezae, Codex, 73

Bloomfield, Paul, 13 n

Booth, General, 159

Brink, C. B., 77 n

Britannica, Encyclopaedia, 144 n

British Broadcasting Corporation, 157

British Council of Churches, 121 n

Brooks, Bishop Phillips, 60

Broomfield, G. W., 77 n

Browne, Sir Thomas, 46

Brunner, Emil, 12

Buber, Martin, 51

Bunyan, John, 138

Burn, Michael, 90 n

Caesarea, 39, 40

Catechisms, 15, 143

Cauter, T., 121 n

Celsus, 41

Charles, R. H., 41, 64, 73 n, 101 n

Charles I, 81

Chemosh, 33

Chesterton, G. K., 51 n

Church Missionary Society, 143

Clough, A. H., 107

Coleraine, Lord, 149

Common Prayer, Book of, 15, 80, 102

Constantine, Emperor, 44

Corinth, 41, 43, 124

Coupland, R. H., 108 n

Cromwell, Oliver, 146

Dagadu, P. K., 106
Daily Prayer Book (Jewish), 117
Dale, R. W., 99
Daniel, 44
Daniell, G. W., 82 n
David, King, 34, 125
Davidman, Joy, vii
Denning, Mr. Justice, 119
Dewar, Lindsay, 129 n, 169
Didache, 139
Diognetus, 117 n
Dodd, C. H., 35, 50
Donaldson, Bishop St. C., 130
Doncaster, 45
Downham, J. S., 121 n
Drewett, John, vii, 136
Driberg, Tom, 157 n

Edersheim, A., 39 n
Egypt, 19, 20, 25, 31, 67, 74, 75, 87, 117, 138
Eichrodt, W., 77 n
Elijah, 51
Elisha, 24, 49
Elizabeth I, 11, 123
Elton, Lord, 158
Emerson, R. W., 151
Ems, 154
Ephesus, 170
Ervine, St. J., 160 n

Flugel, J. C., 14 n
Francis, St. of Assisi, 140
Friends, Society of, 59

Galilee, 39
Gambia, 107

Gandhi, Mahatma, 156, 157
Garbett, Archbishop W., 119 n
Gee, Henry, 12 n
George V., 103
Germany, Western, 71
Ghana, 106, 143
Giornale D'Italia, 156
Glover, T. R., 41 n
Godwin, George, 112 n, 113 n, 167 n
Goldman, Samuel, 12 n, 168
Gollancz, Victor, 69, 70
Goodall, N., 77 n
Gordon, General, 158
Gore, Bishop Charles, 48, 85, 144
Goudge, H. L., 41 n, 80
Green, F. W., 60 n
Gwatkin, H. M., 117 n

Hawkins, W. B., 161 n
Headlam, A. C., 177
Henson, Bishop Hensley, 71
Hereros, 135 ff., 143
Herod, 39
Hezekiah, 35
Hitler, Adolf, 154
Hoare, Sir S. *See* Temple-wood, Lord.
Hodges, H. A., 18, 21
Hodgson, Leonard, 26 n
Hollywood, 118, 121
Home and Family Life, 121 n
Homilies, Book of, 123
Hooker, Richard, 17
Hudson's Bay Company, 134, 135

Inge, W. R., 11
Inter-Church Aid, 109
Ipswich, 45

James I, 81
James, E. O., 124
Jeroboam I, 36
Jerusalem, 40, 125
John, St., 114
Josephus, 40

King, Bishop Edward, 178
Kingsley, Charles, 101 n
Kipling, Rudyard, 13, 17, 75

Latimer, Bishop Hugh, 45
Law, Richard. *See* Coleraine, Lord.
Law, William, 176
Leeds, University of, 91
Leo, Emperor, 45
Lethaby, W. R., 71 n
Loyola, St. Ignatius, 101
Lystra, 49

Macleod, George, 101, 107
Magdalene, St. Mary, 28, 29
Manchester Guardian, 71 n, 91 n, 142, 143, 159
Mandates (Report, 1936), 110
Marriage Guidance Council, 122, 123
Marshall, Dorothy, 16 n
Matthews, W. R., 55
Mazur, Paul, 171 n
Mesha, King, 33
Moffatt, James, 38 n, 42 n
Montefiore, C. G., 148 n

Moore, G. F., 35 n, 39 n
Mumford, Lewis, 152, 173

Naaman, 24
Naomi, 51
National Church and the Social Order, 17 n
Necessity of Art, 173
New Yorker, 174
Nicaea, 46
Nicolson, Sir H., 58, 103 n
Niemöller, Martin, 29, 105
Nigeria, 143

Ober-Ammergau, 170
Oesterley, W. O. E., 17 n
Oxford, Conference on Church Community and State, 30, 104
Origen, 41
Osborn, A. R., 28 n
Ovid, 54

Parker, Archbishop Matthew, 12
Paul, St., 14, 39, 42, 43, 59, 89, 93, 100, 114, 145, 151, 169, 179
Penrice, 45
Phillips, G. E., 35 n
Phillips, J. B., 153 n
Pilate, Pontius, 40
Pompey, 39
Previté-Orton, C. W., 45 n

Ramsay, Sir W., 89
Rawlinson, Bishop A. E. J., 89
Red Sea, 20, 67

Reeves, Marjorie, 174, 175
Richmond, A. H., 78 n
Robertson, C. Grant, 155 n
Robinson, T. H., 17, 86
Robinson, W. Armitage, 139
Roosevelt, Theodore, 144
Rose, J. Holland, 155
Rotterdam, 103
Rowley, H. H., 93 n
Royal Commission on Marriage and Divorce, 120, 122, 123
Ruhr, 103
Ruth, 56

Salvation Army, 159
Samaria, 39
Sanday, W., 177
Scott, C. P., 158, 159
Scott, R. B. Y., 19 n
Sebaste, 39
Serapis, 42
Shakespeare, W., 149
Siéyès, Abbé, 48
Sinai, 19, 20, 31, 36, 68, 126
Söderblom, Archbishop N., 55
Stanley, A. P., 31
Stockholm (Conference), 105
Strachey, Lytton, 159
Stuttgart, 105

Suez, 13, 98
Sweden, 107

Tawney, R. H., 145, 172
Taylor, Jeremy, 83
Taylor, Vincent, 88 n
Temple, Archbishop W., 81, 104, 112
Templewood, Lord, 156, 157 n
Tertullian, 64
Thessalonica, 49
Thompson, Denys, 171 n
Thornton, H., 145
Trevelyan, G. M., 111 n, 112

Veblen, Thorstein, 172
Versailles, Treaty, 105
Vidler, A. C., 176

Wedgwood, Sir J., 129
West Indies, 79
Whitehead, A. N., 26
Whole Duty of Man, 16, 160
Wilberforce, Bishop S., 81
Worcester, 46
World Council of Churches, 30, 104, 105

Zion, 67

Printed in Great Britain
by Wyman & Sons Limited
London · Fakenham · Reading